THE 5

FOUNDATIONS
Of
SUCCESSFUL
TEENS

FAMILIUS

Published by Familius LLC, www.familius.com
Familius books are available at special discounts for bulk purchases, whether
for sales promotions or for family or corporate use. For more information,
contact Familius Sales at 559-876-2170 or email orders@familius.com.

This book is designed to provide information and motivation to our readers.
It is sold with the understanding that it is not engaged to render any type of
psychological, legal, or any other kind of professional advice. No warranties or
guarantees are expressed or implied. Neither the publisher nor the individual
author shall be liable for any physical, psychological, emotional, financial,
or commercial damages, including, but not limited to, special, incidental,
consequential, or other damages. Some names and identifying details have
been changed to protect the privacy of individuals.

Library of Congress Cataloging-in-Publication Data
2018937156
Print ISBN 9781641700375
Ebook ISBN 9781641700887

Printed in the United States of America

Edited by Lindsay Sandberg
Cover design by David Miles
Book design by inlinebooks

10 9 8 7 6 5 4 3 2 1

First Edition

MARK J. LUCIANO, PHD

THE 5

FOUNDATIONS

Of

SUCCESSFUL

TEENS

How to Ignite Your
Underperforming Teen's Self-Reliance
and Academic Success

To all parents who work hard to foster the good things in family life:

love, joy, peace, patience, kindness, gentleness, faithfulness, generosity, and self-control.

CONTENTS

INTRODUCTION   The Challenge-Averse Teen   1

CHAPTER 1   Character Strengths and Parenting Style   9

CHAPTER 2   Authoritative Parenting and Intrinsic Motivation   19

CHAPTER 3   The Five Types   31

CHAPTER 4   The Confidence-Building Teen   37

CHAPTER 5   The Independence-Building Teen   73

CHAPTER 6   The Initiative-Building Teen   99

CHAPTER 7   The Identity-Building Teen   117

CHAPTER 8   The Trust-Building Teen   135

CHAPTER 9   Bottom Line   149

Endnotes   159

Acknowledgments   163

About the Author   165

The Challenge-Averse Teen

R esearch has repeatedly shown that an alarming percentage of our students achieve below their academic ability.[1] It's virtually a national epidemic.

In the United States, about fifty percent of students enrolled in college will never graduate, and the graduation rate is dropping.[2] Across the country, ten to twenty percent of high school dropouts are intellectually gifted.[3] Parents are rightly concerned about their teens' future. According to data released by ACT in 2016, only twenty-five percent of high school graduates have the reading, math, English, and science skills they need to succeed in college or a career.[4] More young adults are now living with their parents than during the Great Recession. According to U.S. Census data, the share of eighteen- to thirty-four-year-olds living with their parents was 31.5 percent as of March 2015. Ten years ago, just 27 percent of young adults lived with their parents.[5]

Are you concerned that your son or daughter is smarter than their grades are reflecting? Are you worried that they have fallen into self-destructive patterns that could influence the rest of their lives? These are the warning signs that have likely brought you to read this book.

In my practice for over thirty years as a psychologist, school psychologist, and education consultant, I have seen over and over that high scores on standardized tests or IQ tests do not exempt teens from emotional and developmental turmoil. It's just a normal part of being a teen.

I remember being a teen quite clearly. When I think about it, I realize it wasn't paradise. Quite the opposite; I was a rather shy introverted kid. My family life was rather dysfunctional. Although I did well in school, it was in spite of my family and social environment—not because of it. Most adults can look back and recall that being a middle-school or high-school aged teen meant all kinds of uncomfortable and downright awkward social situations on top of all the school pressure. And many teens have it tougher today than we did when we were kids! And even if your family doesn't appear to have the typical risk factors, your teenager may still be struggling with developing the key skills and character traits needed to succeed.

All types of academic, emotional, and social challenges are to be expected for teens. In fact, challenges are quite necessary for teens to eventually become successful adults. We'll address more about this later.

I have seen that while most teens can do well in school, some are just not motivated. Many of the teens I have worked with over the years get stuck in a pattern of actively avoiding the ordinary challenges of being a teen. They have become *Challenge Averse*.

This book looks at Challenge-Averse Teens and proven ways for parents to help them succeed.

Common Characteristics

Challenge-Averse Teens share certain characteristics. Here are some of the glaring character traits that develop when teens actively avoid the challenges life puts in front of them:

Challenge-Averse Teens do not function independently. If a parent or teacher supervises a Challenge-Averse Teen, the project will be finished. However, when the parent stops supervising, the teen stops working. They may tackle academic challenges with a tutor, an interested teacher, or a parent, but usually not by themselves.

Challenge-Averse Teens have difficulty finishing projects. They may start many different projects, but will often not finish them. They don't have the persistence to completion in the short term or what we now call grit—the ability to be persistent and passionate over the longer term. How do we help teens develop these qualities? Challenge-Averse Teens do not adhere to time structures and deadlines. They push the limits. They need one more day or one more week. Sometimes, they complete ninety-nine percent of the project, but fail to turn it in.

Most Challenge-Averse Teens are in the average range of intelligence or better. Their academic difficulties are not chiefly due to ADHD or a learning disability, though these conditions may be a factor. Yet, whatever their native ability, Challenge-Averse Teens actively avoid academic challenges.

Challenge-Averse Teens may be described as lazy by parents and teachers. They know that they could do much better in their studies but they don't seem to have the desire to do so. They allow positive opportunities to sail by.

A common misconception is that Challenge-Averse Teens are unmotivated and rudderless. Actually, quite the opposite is true! Although Challenge-Averse Teens procrastinate, lie, and make excuses, all of this behavior serves a particular goal. Challenge-Averse Teens are highly motivated *to avoid success at all costs.*[6]

Causal Factors

What is the root cause of teens actively avoiding and overcoming normal challenges? A Challenge-Averse Teen is afraid of eventually achieving independence. The notion of becoming an independent adult may be provoking anxiety ("If I succeed today, then I will be expected to succeed tomorrow. If I succeed today and tomorrow, I will be expected to succeed for the rest of my life").[7]

Sometimes, birth order is a factor. For example, if an older sibling is doing well in school, the younger brother or sister may consider the older sibling as perfect and give up trying. This occurs because teens want to establish their own identity and be different in some way from their siblings.

In other cases, a teen may compare themselves with their parents' level of success and decide they can't compete. They drop out and decide to do something completely different.

If a parent is successful yet distant, the teen may remain distant and aloof from their parents.

Another factor is the focus on outcomes rather than process. If a teen brings home an A in math, a parent may say, "Great! Let's celebrate and go out to dinner." The Challenge-Averse Teen thinks, "This is pressure to get As in the future." However, the parent can choose to place the focus on the process rather than the outcome, relieving the teen's sense of feeling pressured. The parent could do this by observing, "You look happy about that. You are surprised you could do it." Or, if the Challenge-Averse Teen doesn't appear happy about the good grade, a parent may observe, "Sometimes nothing feels right," which helps the teen to focus on their feelings rather than on the outcome alone.

Our teens today have social media where they see young celebrities, sometimes their own age, who are rock stars, accomplished actors, dancers, geniuses, etc. They look at their friends' social media pages and tend to think, "Gee, my life just isn't as great as theirs." It's really just another example of seeing the outcome as more important than the journey. Yet, it's the journey that counts.

Ineffective Approaches

I have observed parents try all types of shoot-from-the hip approaches that don't work with Challenge-Averse Teens. I have heard parents describe them all.

Tutoring alone does not work. The Challenge-Averse Teen will accept the help as long as a tutor or you are physically with them. They will complete work when doing the work along with the tutor. As soon as the tutor leaves, they stop working and the assignments remain unfinished.

Power tactics do not work. If this is your approach, homework becomes a daily power struggle. Parents tell me they notice whether or not the teen is working on their assignments and become anxious whenever they see that a homework assignment has not been done. Their teen may become anxious and uncomfortable and hide the assignments. It becomes a cat-and-mouse game. The atmosphere of anxiety and awkwardness—sometimes outright anger and rage surrounding the subject of schoolwork—becomes unbearable.

Changing schools or changing to a different classroom usually does not solve the problem. The teen most often does not respond favorably to the new environment. There may be a period during which the teen begins to complete assignments, but soon old patterns begin to reappear.

Rewards don't work by themselves. One father promised his son a new car if he successfully completed his junior year of high school. His son completed his junior year of high school with a B average, then dropped out to enjoy his new car.

The following worksheet can help you identify if your teen is a Challenge-Averse Teen.

Is your teen Challenge Averse? Check all that apply:

1. Scores average or above average on intelligence and end-of-year achievement tests, but receives poor grades.
2. Has difficulty working on their own.
3. Seems unable to spend constructive time alone.
4. Does not apply him/herself.
5. Has a short attention span.
6. Spends much time in nonproductive activity such as surfing the internet, watching TV, playing video games, or "chillin'."
7. Little or no time is spent on assignments or homework.
8. Lies about completing assignments and may hide new assignments.
9. Procrastinates on assignments, major school projects, and chores and usually needs reminders.
10. Doesn't take responsibility for their own actions and may blame others or circumstances for failure.
11. Abandons projects in the middle or loses interest in projects even when started with enthusiasm.
12. Receives poor grades in the major academic subjects but may do well in one subject only. He/she may perform well in PE, art, or music.
13. Performance is usually inconsistent. Does well sometimes but poorly other times.
14. Easily discouraged.
15. Lacks grit, perseverance, stick-to-itiveness and self-discipline.
16. Has high ambitions, but makes no realistic plans for the future.
17. Avoids challenges.
18. Shows a lack of pride in their work.
19. Unable to explain why he/she does poorly.
20. Teachers say he/she is a "great kid," but is simply not motivated.

Evaluating the Challenge-Averse Teen Checklist

Number of YES responses:

1–3	Probably not Challenge Averse.
4–7	Likely to be Challenge Averse.
8–20	Very high probability of being Challenge Averse.

CHAPTER 1

Character Strengths
and
Parenting Style

Progressives and conservatives agree—character strengths are essential ingredients in the recipe for academic and life success. Researchers have even identified specific character traits as the building blocks of "good character." These include grit, self-control, zest, social intelligence, gratitude, optimism, and curiosity.

How do we, as parents, foster these important character traits?

"The best way for a young person to build character is for him to attempt something where there is a real and serious possibility of failure. In a high-risk endeavor, whether it's in business or athletics or the arts, you are more likely to experience colossal defeat than in a low-risk one—but you're also more likely to achieve real and original success. 'The idea of building grit and building self-control is that you get that through failure.'"[1]

But what happens when your teen avoids challenging situations? What if your teen has become Challenge Averse? Recognize that your Challenge-Averse teen is not lazy or unmotivated! Rather, they are highly motivated to achieve the goal of just getting by.

This book is an attempt to answer this important question. Many researchers have recently looked at the "how" of addressing good character development and encouraging young people to fulfill their potential. Let's review what we know.

Character Strengths

Character strengths are known as non-cognitive or "soft" skills. These character strengths have been a growing area of interest for researchers in the area of child and adolescent development. The evidence shows unstable environments can create biological changes in the growing brains of children and adolescents. Those changes impair the development of the so-called executive functions of the developing brain. Executive functions are the skills that help young people regulate their thoughts and feelings, process information effectively, and manage emotions in such a way that they can succeed in school and in life.

I explain the basic idea behind "executive function" quite simply as "telling yourself what to do." My famous saying with teens I have worked with over the years is, "If you don't tell yourself what to do, someone else is very likely to come along and do it for you." And I practice what I preach. I find that talking to myself or giving myself directions is a good idea. For example, I find the best way to remember a phone number is to repeat the numbers to myself over and over until I can dial the number. This is really a way to enhance one's short-term working memory skills. In graduate school, I was selected for the demonstration of a visual spatial test in front of the whole class. The task involved selecting the correct design to fit as part of another design. You had to mentally rotate the image to find the correct answer. I found "talking myself through" the task to be the most effective way to do it ("This looks like the mirror image . . . I should turn this around . . . the top right goes with the bottom left . . .").

It helped to talk to myself to organize my approach ("Do this first. Do that next . . . Now what?"). Then, I answer the question and follow my own instructions. In part, executive function is like the executive in your head directing the action.

Long-term psychological studies show that young people who demonstrate these non-cognitive executive skills do well in school and later in life ("Executive function and self-regulation skills are the mental processes that enable teens to plan, focus attention, remember instructions, and juggle multiple tasks successfully. Just as an air traffic control system at a busy airport safely manages the arrivals and departures of many aircraft on multiple runways, the brain needs this skill set to filter distractions, prioritize tasks, set and achieve goals, and control impulses").[2]

The well-known Stanford marshmallow experiment was a series of studies on delayed gratification (i.e., self-control) in the late 1960s and early 1970s led by psychologist Walter Mischel, a professor at Stanford University. The important executive function of self-control was investigated with young children. In these studies, a child was offered a choice between one small reward provided immediately or two small rewards if they waited for approximately fifteen minutes, during which the tester left the room and then returned.

The researchers found that children who were able to wait longer by using various self-control strategies tended to have better life outcomes as measured by SAT scores, educational attainment, and other measures.

In another long-term study conducted in New Zealand in the early 1970s, kids with strong, non-cognitive executive skills were more likely to finish school and have better health, and were less likely to have credit or legal problems or become single parents.

Research into self-control as a non-cognitive skill unites all the social and behavioral sciences. Self-control is really an overarching concept which includes the non-cognitive skills of conscientiousness, self-regulation, delay of gratification, attentiveness, executive function, and willpower. Neuroscientists who study self-control as an executive function served by the brain's frontal cortex have uncovered brain structures and systems involved when research participants exert self-control.

What Parents Need to Know

Do we as parents need to know *all* the research and brain chemistry behind the importance of character strengths for our kids' future? No, but it helps to know the link between Character Strengths and later success is clearly revealed by research.

A much more important question is: Does research point to *how* we, as parents, can nurture the development of Character Strengths important for success in school and in life? The answer, happily, is yes.

Character Strengths cannot really be directly taught as, say, math skills. They may be most accurately seen as a product of a young person's environment. As parents, we have the ability to influence the development of these important skills over time. There is strong evidence this is true of early childhood, and there is growing evidence that in middle and high school kids', character strengths are a reflection of their environment.

You can't teach character by just telling kids to be more confident or self-assured or have more intellectual courage. The way kids learn that is by continually being compelled and supported to accept risks and challenges.[3]

Here is the equation: Character Strengths are needed for long-term success. Character Strengths are a reflection of a teen's environment. Character Strengths are a product of teens being consistently encouraged and supported in accepting reasonable risk and challenge.

As I asked earlier, what happens when a teen is very much averse to challenging situations?

The answer lies in providing the consistent family (and school) environment to encourage your teen to accept risk and challenge. Not too much risk and challenge; not too little. You have to find the "Goldilocks Zone."

What's needed is a consistent environment that encourages and supports your teen in *accepting reasonable challenges*.

Family Environment and Parenting Style

How do we, as parents, build such an environment at home?

The vast majority of research has found parenting style to be important as a foundation and a consistent predictor of positive outcomes. The research overwhelmingly indicates that parenting behaviors such as *parental warmth* and *parental rules* are associated with positive outcomes.[4]

What are these two elements, parental warmth and parental rules?

Diane Baumrind is a researcher who proposed a system for classifying parenting types.[5] She looked at two specific factors: parental warmth (empathy/support) and behavioral rules/limits. Here are the three classifications that we will use throughout the book:

Permissive Parents provide lots of warmth, empathy, and support for their kids. But Permissive Parents are reluctant to impose rules and standards. They prefer to let their kids regulate themselves.

Authoritarian Parents provide behavioral limits, rules, and discipline, but not as much warmth, empathy, and support.

Authoritative Parents provide high levels of both behavioral limits and parental support. They set high behavioral requirements. In addition, they provide a nurturing and responsive family environment. They respect teens as independent and able to make decisions.

Notice the subtle but critical difference in the labels "Authoritarian" and "Authoritative."

Authoritative Parents expect good behavior and cooperation. They offer consistent emotional support, especially when their teen is stressed. Like Permissive Parents, they are nurturing and responsive to their teen. However, *unlike* Permissive Parents, they do not let kids get away with poor behavior. Like Authoritarian Parents, they provide lots of rules and limits. *Unlike* Authoritarian Parents, they provide much support and warmth. Authoritative Parents are both highly responsive and very demanding.[6]

Looking at the Three Parenting Styles

James and Lisa are Permissive Parents. They are very warm and positive with their teenage son, Jarod, and are rather undemanding. For example, they allow Jarod, thirteen, to set his bedtime for anytime he wants. He stays up late a lot on weeknights watching television and playing video games. James and Lisa don't mind Jarod setting his own schedule. They believe he will eventually learn on his own to get to bed earlier because he'll feel tired the next day. They don't remind him about chores or homework either.

James and Lisa are generally passive in their parenting. They believe the way to demonstrate their love is to let Jarod do pretty much whatever he wants. If Jarod wants a new video game, James just takes him to buy it as soon as he asks. James and Lisa are very much available to talk with Jarod and spend time with him.

Permissive Parents invoke such phrases as, "Sure, you can stay up late if you want to," and "You do not need to do any chores if you don't feel like it." They are more responsive to their teen and less demanding. They are nontraditional and lenient, do not require mature behavior, and avoid confrontation. They want their teen's friendship and approval.

Permissive Parents do not like to say "no" or disappoint their teen. As a result, teens are allowed to make many important decisions without parental input. Permissive Parents do not view themselves as active participants in shaping their teen's actions. Rather, they view themselves as an available resource if he chooses to seek their advice.

Frank and Gina are Authoritarian Parents. They love Ben, their fifteen-year-old son; yet, they are not "touchy feely" parents, so they don't hug him often. They are strict disciplinarians and use a restrictive, somewhat punitive style. They insist Ben follow their directions. They believe strict rules are necessary for kids. It had always been that way in both of their homes when they grew up. If the rules are violated, a punishment is imposed. For example, when Ben stayed out a half hour over his ten p.m. curfew for the first time, he was grounded for two weeks. Frank and Gina are consistent with their enforcement of their house rules.

Authoritarian Parents invoke phrases such as, "You will do this because I said so," and "Because I'm the parent, and you are not." Authoritarian Parents do not engage in discussions with their teen, and family rules and standards are not debated.

Authoritarian Parents believe kids should accept, without question, the rules and practices that they establish. Authoritarian Parents are highly demanding and directive, but not as responsive. They are obedience- and status-oriented, and they expect their orders to be obeyed without explanation. They provide well-ordered and structured environments with clearly stated rules.

Research reveals that teens of Authoritarian Parents learn that following parental rules and adherence to strict discipline is valued over independent behavior. As a result, teens may become either too rebellious or too dependent. Those who become rebellious might display aggressive behaviors. Teens who are more submissive tend to remain dependent on their parents.

Authoritative Parents use a more balanced approach.

David and Lilly are Authoritative Parents. They are open to discuss their rules with their seventeen-year-old daughter, Kayla. They tell her the reasoning behind their policies and are willing to discuss her objections when she complains. Yet, they make it clear that they will make the final decision. Kayla told her parents she wanted to go to a rock concert with a group of friends. David and Lilly were concerned. At first, they gave her a flat "no." Kayla complained that she would be left out of the best event of the fall. David and Lilly asked several questions about the situation and the particular friends who would be in the group. They researched the band and the venue on the internet. After a lengthy discussion, they insisted on Kayla following a number of conditions, including checking in by calling them at the end of the show. They discussed the transportation arrangements. They gave her guidelines ("Stay with your group"). On these conditions, they gave their approval.

Authoritative Parents affirm the teen's qualities and also set standards for future conduct. They use reason and discussion to set their policies. They do not base decisions on consensus or solely on the teen's desires. Authoritative Parents are warm, but firm. They encourage their teen to be independent while maintaining limits and controls on their actions.

Authoritative Parents do not invoke the "Because I said so" rule. Instead, they are willing to entertain, listen to, and take into account their teen's viewpoint. They engage in discussions and even debates with their teens, although ultimate responsibility for setting limits resides with the parents.

Authoritative Parenting supports Character Strength development. Research demonstrates that teens of Authoritative Parents learn how to negotiate and engage in discussions. They understand that their opinions are valued. They emotionally feel closer to their parents, yet are more autonomous and independent as well. They develop a sense of competence in the family environment. As a result, they are more likely to be socially competent, responsible, and autonomous in the school environment.

Authoritative Parenting is associated with healthy development. It provides a balance between affection and support on the one hand and an appropriate level of parental rules on the other. This atmosphere provides opportunities for the teen to become self-reliant and to develop a healthy sense of autonomy within a set of parental limits, guidelines, and rules.

Differing Parenting Styles

What if parents differ in their styles of parenting? When parenting styles differ, it can be frustrating, yet it is very common. Even parents who have read a lot of parenting books find that they lean one way or another—Permissive or Authoritarian—in various situations. That's because your parenting style is influenced by the way your parents raised you and the way you responded to them. Even when you and your partner differ, it doesn't have to be a disaster. In fact, your teen will benefit from learning how to deal with your different parenting styles.

In practice, your teen may attempt to take advantage of your differences. So, it is important parents discuss the significant rules fully and reach a consensus between the two of you before discussing them with your teen. Since you are individuals, you will naturally handle situations quite differently. And it's OK to be different. Sometimes, agreeing to disagree is necessary. Compromise can also be a good thing. If parenting differences are becoming chronic or if you and your partner fight frequently about parenting, seek some counseling about the issue. Always aim for consistency in setting rules in specific recurrent situations. This consistency is important for your child, as well as for your relationship.

Also, be aware that teen behavior influences parenting style. Whereas a cooperative, motivated, and responsible teen may be more likely to have parents who exercise an Authoritative Parenting style, an uncooperative and irresponsible teen may be more likely to elicit a parenting style that is more Authoritarian, Permissive, or uninvolved.

Remember, Challenge-Averse Teens are not lazy and unmotivated; they are highly motivated to achieve the goal of just getting by. They are successfully achieving what they set out to do—which is to just get by in school and at home—so they can avoid more responsibility and avoid facing the future. In such a situation, a major part of the parental responsibility is to create a system for having open communication with the student's teachers so that all information regarding upcoming assignments and exams is readily available. But more about this later.

Let your teen know that you will be informed, so you will be able to do regular checks of their school work. This includes asking to see the work so you know whether it was or was not done.

Eventually—with patient and proper intervention—the goal is for the Challenge-Averse Teen to own the problem, not for you, as parents, to take responsibility. The student may receive assistance with assignments, but parents should not be more invested in the assignment being completed than the student.

It is of the utmost importance to tailor your efforts as a parent to your teen and their individual needs. Research supports the notion that personality and the parent–child relationship is a two-way street.

Your teen may naturally be easier or more difficult for you to handle as a parent. For example, a so-called strong-willed teen may challenge a more gentle-spirited parent to become more assertive. By the same token, a sweet-natured teen may present a challenge for more high-energy, decisive parents to modulate and tone down their approach.

This book provides some helpful stories, practical advice, and valuable input to effectively recognize your teen's unique and individual qualities and effectively organize your thoughtful response as parents to provide a family environment that will help develop the character strengths your teen needs to succeed in school and in life.

Let's take a closer look at how Authoritative Parenting can set up a consistent environment that encourages and supports Challenge-Averse Teens in accepting reasonable challenges.

CHAPTER 2

Authoritative Parenting and Intrinsic Motivation

C hallenge-Averse Teens benefit from a consistent family environment in which they are encouraged and supported to face reasonable challenges—even when they don't want to.

Homework Time

One of the first actions I advise parents to do is to set up a specific homework time each day. Most often, it is one hour in the afternoon before dinner. Every situation is different, but generally kids like to get home and unwind for a while (like adults). The discussion with your teen usually involves agreeing to set an hour or so to relax and then a specific time, say four to five p.m., for homework time. The rule for homework time, of course, is no electronics, entertainment, social media, smartphones, or any interruptions. Only doing homework or studying.

What's in it for the teen? You, as parents, promise not to mention schoolwork at any other time of day. It's a good deal for everyone. Your teen most probably believes she is constantly nagged about homework and school (even if this is an exaggeration). And you could use a break from thinking about it. I have found that focusing the issue of academic work down to just one hour a day is really helpful. For the rest of the day, parents can let it go.

The truth is that parents are often as anxious about their kid's failing grades as the teen is—whether your teen acknowledges anxiety or not. This can make for a very tense home situation. So, letting go of the issue for twenty-three of the twenty-four hours in a day can help. You are not ignoring the issue. Just focus the issue to one hour.

Implementing the Rule

If our goal is to develop an environment where kids are consistently supported and encouraged to face challenges, the homework-time rule is a great place to start. Why? School accomplishment is, of course, one of the most important challenges for teens.

When Chris, a fifteen-year-old, got home from school, his mother noticed he went straight to his room to post a meme he had created on his Facebook page and check his YouTube channel for the number of hits his posted videos had received. That was OK since the agreed upon homework time started at four p.m. When four p.m. rolled around, he was still watching YouTube music videos that his mom could hear from outside his closed door.

Chris's mom became instantly annoyed. She had been working on not yelling or even raising the intensity level at times like this. She paused and told herself, "OK. I'm going to calm myself down first, so I can approach this in the best way possible. I want to maintain my cool, so that I'm coming across as Authoritative, not Authoritarian."

(Of course, she had been working in counseling along with Chris's dad and had learned the parenting theory. Now, it was time to put the theory into action!)

She knocked on his door and said, "Why haven't you started your homework time?" in a voice loud enough to be heard over the video, but not in an irritated tone. She immediately thought to herself, "I did that well. I'm calm, firm, and level-headed."

Chris replied, "Mom, I'm downloading my English chapter, so chill. Get off my back."

She ignored the snarky comeback and said, "Chris, I understand you are downloading the English text, but this is homework time, so use the wait time to do another assignment or some reading. It's only one hour." She smiled and left.

Chris groaned, but shut off YouTube and started reading a text book.

The Authoritative Environment

Chris's mom used an Authoritative Parenting approach. Notice the Authoritative approach brought the challenge directly to Chris; in this case, following an agreement he had willingly entered into about getting his homework done even though he did not want to live up to the agreement at that moment in time. For her part, Chris's mom was not confrontational, but matter-of-fact. She simply asked "Why haven't you started your homework time?" directly referring to the agreement they both knew Chris had entered into willingly.

As we have observed, the Authoritative Parenting approach is respectful of the teen as an individual who can make and live up to agreements. The older a teen gets, the less rewards and consequences are useful. Rather, *agreements* are a better way to look at the relationship. The teen agrees to do this. I, as a parent, agree to do something in response. I take my responsibility as a parent. I expect my kid to take responsibility also. If he does not, I will thoughtfully respond as a responsible parent.

My Family's Experience

My wife, Shelley and I had a policy of keeping a quiet homework time from about four to five p.m. We modeled this by shutting off the television, radio, and all electronics in the home. Of course, this time changed over the years and was adapted for our four kids, depending on sports practices, schedules, etc. When one of our kids began to have an issue with missing assignments in middle school, we had to adapt to the specific needs. We made sure to know which assignments were due. Shelley and I discussed a thoughtful, assertive response to the situation. It turned out the best way to handle it was rather direct. Since one of us did the pickup from school each day, the rule was, "Don't come into the car unless you have your book and homework." And both of us remembered to check ("Got your book? Do you know your assignments?"). We knew. A few times we had to wait in the car several minutes while the book was retrieved from a school locker.

Authoritarian and Permissive Approaches

If Chris's mom were using the Authoritarian Parenting approach, she would have punished him for his breaking the homework rule and yelled at Chris for his behavior. She wouldn't have considered his defense (downloading his text) and would not have addressed it. The rule was violated, so punishment would be forthcoming. Part of the Authoritarian environment is a lower level of warmth, support, and relationship-building, so Chris would be more likely to resent the punishment and less motivated to cooperate.

If Chris's mom were using the Permissive Parenting approach, she would have spoken with Chris positively and may have reminded him of the rule. However, she would have avoided addressing their prior agreement and giving him a clear direction as she did (telling him, "Chris, don't forget that it's homework time!" and then leaving him alone without following up). Part of the Permissive environment is a lack of follow-through and assertiveness, so Chris would have simply blown her off and gone back to his videos.

If Chris's mom were an uninvolved parent, she wouldn't have a rule about homework at all. Chris would be a kid who lives on the internet and does mostly whatever he wants.

Authoritative Parenting can be difficult at times. It requires being selective about when to intervene, being available and aware of your teen's behavior without hovering, and being realistic about the fact that teens are not perfectly compliant. Flexibility is required so your family life isn't tense and negative. Prioritize the significant issues. Consistency is important. The warmth and support elements are equally important. Keep a positive and caring relationship. Authoritarian rule doesn't inspire good behavior—it just alienates.

Permissive Parents want their teen's approval and love, but they do not assert themselves, sometimes for fear of their teen's negative— sometimes scathing—response. Permissive Parents cave in or are inconsistent. Sometimes super-busy parents appear neglectful because they don't spend the time necessary to meet the sometimes heavy responsibility of being a parent.

The most important elements of Authoritative Parenting—warmth, reasonable rules, and effective communication encouraging autonomy— require energy, focus, and consistency. This warmth and communication leads to natural acceptance, support, and responsiveness. Teens who live in this kind of environment feel they can count on their parents. They see their parents as loving and reasonable.

Parents who have high, but realistic expectations get the best results and naturally present their teen with reasonable challenges quite regularly. When a teen makes mistakes, their focus can safely be on learning rather than expecting a harsh punishment. The situation is discussed and a new agreement is made. If the teen did not live up to the last agreement, the new agreement includes an assertive response from the parent.

Effective communication and encouragement of independence is the third necessary element. Authoritative Parents listen to their teen's views and encourage some give-and-take in negotiations. The ultimate reason for rules and parental authority is, after all, service—to help kids become happy adults, not to micromanage them. Agreements are made to benefit and teach the teen more and more responsibility and independent skill over time. The emphasis of communication is on positive *behavior*.

As an Authoritative Parent, you recognize that the thoughts, opinions, and beliefs are the teen's alone. You have influence with your teen, but not ultimate control. As a parent, you cannot control a teen's behaviors—you can only actively respond to them. A teen's thoughts, feelings, and beliefs are their God-given province. Let them go. Your influence and example are powerful enough.

My Family's Experience

When Shelley and I discussed the missing assignments problem with our teen, we saw that forgetfulness was an element. That's why we decided the new arrangement was needed. In this case, it was, "Don't come into the car unless you have your book and assignments." It worked because we had direct influence at that moment. The car wouldn't move unless the book and assignments were there!

I make it sound easy in hindsight, but we didn't come to this plan of action right away. At first, we simply used reminders and offered small rewards ("When your homework is done we can play a game . . ."). It turned out that, half of the time, the book wasn't in her backpack so our daughter couldn't do the homework, willing or not.

When we saw these ways of addressing the issue were not working, we had to switch gears. We needed an action-oriented plan. How could we be assertive about this important issue without coming across as Authoritarian, heavy-handed, and coercive?

The rule, "Do not get in the car until you have your book and you know your assignment" was not our first thought. And it required action on our part: to remember each day to take the time to check if the book and assignments were there. But this was the most appropriate solution because this response fit with the principle of emphasizing learning (in this case, the skill of remembering important things) rather than punishment for the sake of punishment. The response addressed the problem itself ("We can't go home unless you remembered the important stuff").

The Three Essential Conditions for Encouraging Intrinsic Motivation

An Authoritative Parenting approach predicts teen competence, school performance, emotional maturity, and self-reliance. Why exactly? What does the research say?

Sometimes, young people may make choices in direct opposition to their self-interest—choices that adversely affect the likelihood of reaching their goals, rendering those goals far more difficult to attain. It's puzzling and frustrating to watch. What do social scientists say about this?

Alfred Adler (1870–1937) was a world-renowned philosopher and psychiatrist. He was the first to develop a holistic theory of personality, and he postulated that each individual creates a cognitive "schema," which serves as the individual's reference for attitudes, behaviors, and one's view of self, others, and the world. He believed the growth of confidence, pride, and gratification would naturally lead to a desire and ability to cooperate with others. This feeling of genuine security, he taught, is rooted in a deep sense of belonging and is an intrinsic part of the stream of social evolution.

Also of note, Carl Rogers (1902–1987) was an influential psychologist who developed Person-Centered Therapy. He believed every person can achieve their goals, potential, and desires in life.

He researched the emotional conditions needed for healthy development. These conditions included empathy (feeling understood), acceptance (feeling accepted and respected), and genuineness (openness and self-disclosure). I met Carl Rogers when I was in graduate school. He was as genuine and warm in person as he appeared in video and film.

In the 1970s, Edward Deci and Richard Ryan built on some of these ideas at the University of Rochester. They developed Self-Determination Theory (SDT) as an important theory of motivation that addresses issues of extrinsic and intrinsic motivation and helps to explain why teens make such puzzling choices. They reasoned that people are motivated not only by the *external material rewards* of their actions, but by the *internal enjoyment* and sense of meaning their actions can bring. Deci and Ryan called these internal rewards intrinsic motivation.[1]

They hypothesized people have three innate psychological needs—Relatedness, Autonomy, and Competence. Deci and Ryan contended that intrinsic motivation can only be sustained when people feel that those needs are being satisfied. They conducted a series of experiments to demonstrate that external material rewards are not only ineffective in motivating kids, but can also be counterproductive.

Consider how external rewards effected behavior in a behavioral study done by Deci and Ryan: Two groups were asked to complete challenging and interesting puzzles. Neither of the two groups received rewards for their puzzle-solving. On the second day, one of the groups was told they would be paid a small amount. On the third day, the group that was paid was told the money was gone and they would no longer be paid.

Over the course of the three days, the group that was never paid grew gradually more engaged by the puzzles, simply because they were interesting, and each day, they got a bit faster at completing them. They even kept working on the puzzles over time, increasing their efforts up to and including the third day.

The group that was paid on day two, but unpaid on day three acted differently. On the second day, they worked harder and faster, trying to earn more money. On the third day, when the money stopped, they mostly ignored the puzzles. They worked on them less than when they were being paid and even less than on the first day. The introduction of external rewards had turned the once intrinsically interesting puzzle-solving into a job. Apparently, they didn't want to do the job if they were not going to get paid.[2]

Other researchers replicated this finding. A Stanford psychologist worked with a group of young children who liked to draw. They were told they would get a reward—a blue ribbon—at the end of the class for drawing some pictures, and they received the reward. Two weeks later, they were less interested in drawing. They were also less likely to choose to draw during free time. Drawing had become something worth doing only if there was a blue-ribbon reward offered.

Deci and Ryan believed kids are natural learners. They are born both creative and curious. Intrinsic motivation is equally natural. Many of the tasks students are required to complete at school are not inherently fun or satisfying, but overall motivation to learn new skill and satisfaction when a new skill is mastered is entirely natural. Offering an incentive for the more tedious parts of learning a new complex skill (like memorizing multiplication tables or spelling words) can be a good idea to incentivize boring or repetitive practice. However, in the long run, it is important for students to internalize motivation. When parents and teachers are able to create an environment that promotes feelings of Relatedness, Autonomy, and Competence, teens exhibit much higher levels of *intrinsic* motivation.

And how do parents create that kind of environment? Teens feel a sense of Relatedness when they perceive that their parents like, value, and respect them. Teens experience Autonomy when their parents emphasize a sense of choice while minimizing feelings of coercion and control. Teens feel Competent when their parents give them tasks that they can succeed at but are not too easy—reasonable challenges just beyond their current abilities.

When teens run into trouble, either academically or behaviorally, Authoritarian Parents respond by imposing more control on them, not less, further decreasing their sense of Autonomy. If a teen falls behind peers academically, they feel less Competent. If they are in trouble behaviorally, they feel less Competent and less Relatedness in their family.

When the relationship with their parents is tense or contentious, they feel alienated. Once a teen reaches a point of feeling alienated, no collection of material incentives or punishments will motivate them.

The three feelings or conditions of Relatedness, Autonomy, and Competence—according to Deci and Ryan—are more effective motivators for teens than any external or material reward. If parents want a motivated teen, they need to adjust their family environment and parenting style to promote those feelings.

You will never regret spending extra time with each of your kids *individually* doing what your teen wants to do—even if it's not what you think of as fun and even if you think you are too busy to do it. What is more important, in the end, than spending time with the people you love? Since life is made up of moments, it is important to spend those moments wisely. My personal resolution—that I have never regretted—is to spend time whenever my kids want to spend time with me doing whatever they want to do. When I think I don't have enough time, I remember the saying: "Nobody on their deathbed has ever said, 'I wish I had spent more time at the office.'"[3] My kids have gotten me to do things I never would do and lots of things I now love: hike in the blazing hot Sierra Nevadas in the middle of summer, attempt to surf, watch anime, play "deck building" card and board games, read the New York Times, do yoga, watch soccer, listen to new country music.

There are two very useful ideas I want to introduce at this point: the Connection Response and the 100 Percent Responsibility Rule.

The Connection Response

The Connection Response is the major response that we use with Challenge-Averse Teens. The Connection Response uses reflective listening to acknowledge the feelings that underlie words and encourage teens to think of other situations in which they may have felt the same way.

But the Connection Response is more than simply restating your teen's feelings. It seeks to clarify the feeling content *and* encourage more insight into their thought process in similar situations. It is not simply reflective listening, because a Connection Response also includes inspiring self-reflection, awareness of unconscious issues, and past experiences. The Connection Response helps your teen to fully acknowledge the feelings that underlie their words and gain insight into other situations in which they may have felt a similar way. In turn, this helps your teen to gain insight and mindfulness of their thoughts, feelings, and issues.

Being a good listener means focusing attention on the person speaking and refraining from formulating an answer. The entire focus is on the speaker. A Connection Response can help the teen with their own feelings and understand that you, as a parent, are making that connection as well. But more about this later when we apply the Connection Response in several situations.

The 100 Percent Responsibility Rule

The Rule is simple, but the application is nuanced. The 100 Percent Responsibility Rule is this: Take all of your responsibility, take *none* of theirs. Easy, right? In the realm of parenting a Challenge-Averse Teen, the application of the rule can be complex. The question becomes, "What is my responsibility as a parent in this situation?" and "What is my teen's responsibility?" The answer depends on a number of factors. Most important is to take into account your teen's current abilities.

Can they do this on their own? How much help do they need? The general principle here is "If they can do it, don't do it for them!" Why? It is part of presenting Goldilocks Zone challenges: not too difficult, not too easy. As all parents know, teens (and all kids) are learning all the time. The answer is a moving target as time and circumstance change.

The 100 Percent Responsibility Rule is reminiscent of the old saying, "You can lead a horse to water, but you can't make 'em drink." I would add, "If you try to make them drink, the horse will buck and it will make matters worse." More about this later also when we apply the 100 Percent Responsibility Rule in a number of diverse situations.

Now, let's meet each of the Five Types of Challenge-Averse Teens.

CHAPTER 3

The Five Types

As I have observed, there are five particular types of Challenge-Averse Teens. Of course, each person is an individual with a unique personality. Here are a few stories of kids who underperform.

At fourteen years old, Jon learned that it is better to say nothing than to try to explain his ideas. He was able to hide a learning disability with his creative sleight of hand and his high level of intelligence. He slid by until seventh grade, when the text and vocabulary requirements became too difficult for him due to his learning disability. Jon had no trouble understanding high-level concepts. Yet, he did not complete homework and usually got poor grades. He began isolating himself from others. He was still curious and intelligent, but Jon had difficulty explaining his thoughts to teachers, whom he saw as critical and mean.

Instead of talking, Jon filled his notebook with drawings of characters from science fiction and comics. On weekends, he would stay in his room going on Facebook and Snapchat, creating memes and watching short videos.

Carlos is a fifteen-year-old young man with brown hair, brown eyes, and disheveled clothes usually a few sizes too big. He was withdrawn and shy, but often short and disrespectful with teachers and his parents. He began to hang out with a "bad crowd" and frequently cut afternoon classes to meet up with his friends. At home, his father drank a lot and his parents argued about the issue of alcohol abuse. Carlos referred to his father as a "dick" when talking about him with peers. His grades began to slide when he entered high school.

Anthony is a seventeen-year-old who loves to skateboard and binge-watch television shows. He occasionally smokes pot but doesn't consider it a problem. He has fallen behind in high school credits and has been asked by the school administration to make up the credits, online so he would be in range to graduate just a year late if he attended summer classes. Even though he is in danger of not graduating high school, he appears unconcerned. He projects a "mellow" personality, seldom initiating conversation with adults, but is quite popular with peers.

Diana is a sixteen-year-old who was identified by her school district as "gifted" in the fifth grade after receiving high IQ scores. She came from a family of high achievers, including her sister who was accepted to an Ivy League college. Her grades were good in elementary school, but she began to have difficulty when she entered the sixth grade. Her grades plummeted from As and Bs to Cs and Ds. In the eighth grade, Diana was removed from advanced classes as a result of poor grades. Her academic difficulty continued through the first years of high school. When her parents expressed their concern about her grades, she claimed that many of her friends were failing classes. She focused on her interest in ecology and "saving the planet." She received good grades in classes that interested her, such as environmental science.

Throughout early elementary school, Sofia was near the top of her class. She finished her work before other students and helped peers, despite the fact that her parents constantly fought. She created a top project at the science fair. When she turned seventeen, Sofia's life changed after her parents divorced. She moved to a new neighborhood and hung around with an entirely different set of friends. Her mother, Jocelyn, took on a second job, requiring Sofia to care for her two young brothers. With the added responsibility, she often arrived late to school. She would fall asleep during second period. Her friends helped to fill in the void. As Sofia's grades dropped, she lost all interest in academics.

Five Types of Challenge-Averse Teens

There are five types of Challenge-Averse Teens roughly corresponding to Erik Erikson's Psychosocial Stages of Development.[1] Of course, not all teens fit neatly into one type. Some appear to have features of more than one.

The Confidence-Building Teen is a young person experiencing distress—that is, anxiety about performing well and/or depression and sadness. Young people manifest anxiety and depression differently than adults. Often, anxiety and depression are not readily apparent and are instead manifested as behavioral symptoms. The Confidence-Building Teen may want to perform well, but may become overwhelmed with beginning assignments or studying for a test. They succumb to procrastination to avoid the anxiety of facing the situation. The Confidence-Building Teen may constantly worry about becoming competent. They are generally perfectionists and may waste time worrying about details of an assignment to the point that the task will not be completed.

The Independence-Building Teen lives for the moment. He or she is impulsive and generally wants instant gratification. The Independence-Building Teen may generally underperform as a way to rebel against authority. They are generally defiant and quite crafty. An Independence-Building Teen will copy assignments and readily cheat on tests. They effortlessly lie, regularly cut classes, and manipulate others artfully to get exactly what they want. They relish beating the system and making authority look foolish. However, they may also display hostility and may blame others for their own mistakes and underachievement.

The Initiative-Building ("Easygoing") teen doesn't generally show anger or hostility, but floats through life taking the path of least resistance. They don't take the initiative. Superficially, the mellow teen appears unconcerned about schoolwork. They procrastinate and make excuses. They maintain the façade of indifference. Under the façade, however, the Initiative-Building Teen is just as anxious and concerned about their future as other teens.

The Identity-Building Teen is focused on figuring out who they are and what they believe. These young people are aware of social issues. They experiment with different styles of dress and different groups of friends. They may believe that other family members are too successful to compete with, so they drop out of the competition. They explore where they might belong in the larger society. They generally have no clear plan of action or path but express their ideas passionately as a way to define their beliefs as quite distinct from their parents'.

The Trust-Building Teen is a youth who has experienced stressful and significant life changes, which have resulted in symptoms of depression and anxiety. Basic trust has been compromised in his or her young life. When there is significant stress—a divorce, an alcoholic or addicted parent, or another major event has occurred in his or her life—a teen may become withdrawn or not cope well with the situation. These teens may become unable to meet the challenges of adolescence as a result.

Each of the teens introduced above are a representative of each type.

Jon is a Confidence-Building Teen. He learned to "lay low" and say nothing rather than explain his ideas. Because he is smart, he was able to hide a learning disability for a long time. His parents had him as-sessed in seventh grade after text and vocabulary requirements became too difficult for him due to the learning disability. While he had learned to read by simply memorizing sight words, he had very poor skills decoding unfamiliar new words. The assessment showed that Jon had difficulty with auditory processing and decoding unfamiliar words. However, he had no trouble understanding high-level concepts. It was just that his ability to demonstrate his knowledge in writing had fallen behind grade level. He began feeling discouraged and isolated from others. With his continued frustration, he stopped completing his homework and received poor grades. Because Jon saw his teachers as critical and mean, he had difficulty explaining his thoughts and ideas. Even after Jon received appropriate intervention and extra help for his learning differences, he continued to bring home poor grades. The experience of falling behind had taken a toll; he had become anxious, depressed, and averse to taking on academic challenge.

Carlos is an Independence-Building Teen. He's the one who had begun to hang out with a "bad crowd" and frequently cut afternoon classes to meet up with his friends. His father drank, and Carlos was quite critical of him. He brought home Ds and Fs and had also begun to refer to his father as a "dick." In counseling sessions with me, Carlos would wind up complaining about his dad and his parents' fighting, and would question the usefulness of school and counseling. "You're just making money off my parents," he'd accuse. Before one session, Carlos's mother told me he had locked her out of the house and wouldn't let her back in for two hours. When I asked Carlos about what he had done, he denied doing it ("My mom's crazy").

Anthony is an Initiative-Building ("Easygoing") Teen. As far as he was concerned, there really was no problem. Sure, he was a little behind in school. Who wasn't? "No need to get upset," he'd say. His parents were much more concerned about his academic underperformance than he appeared to be. They had spent time and money attempting to arrange a summer class at an expensive non-public school so he could make up his deficient credits. Anthony, for his part, went along with attending the summer class but didn't finish the assignments. His parents' efforts were wasted. Anthony just shrugged. He said he had done his best and it wasn't a big deal. In reality, underneath his calm and uncaring attitude, Anthony was quite anxious about his future. He avoided academic challenges precisely because it was easier to coast around them than to face the possibility of failure.

Diana is an Identity-Building Teen. Although she came from a family of high achievers, she was not interested in applying herself at school. She spent her time talking with older friends who were involved in soliciting funds for Greenpeace. She worked diligently on art projects related to Ecology. Although she obtained a high IQ score and her grades were relatively good in elementary school, her grades plummeted when she entered middle school and into high school. However, she received good grades in Environmental Science and claimed she would pursue a degree after she had some "life experience." Diana's focus was on developing her independent interests, rather than investing her time and effort in areas where she felt compared to her sister or parents.

Sofia is a Trust-Building Teen. Her life changed completely when her parents divorced. She moved to a new neighborhood and hung around with an entirely different set of friends. Her mother had taken on a second job as a newly single parent, so she was not around in the afternoon when Sofia got out of school. Sofia was required to be in the apartment when her two young brothers got home from school until her mom got home. Her friends helped to fill in the void. She was home every afternoon, but often left to go out with friends as soon as her mom arrived. She stayed out late, even on weeknights, and she often arrived late to school. Sofia lost all interest in academics and said she wanted to drop out of high school. The stress of the significant changes was too much for Sofia to handle.

Now, let's look more closely at each of the Five Types.

CHAPTER 4

The Confidence-Building Teen

When Jon's history teacher asked him to write a report about Franklin Roosevelt, before putting pen to paper Jon came up with endless questions:

"Should the report be on yellow paper or white?"

"How long should it be?"

"How many sources are supposed to be in the bibliography?"

"Should I discuss Eleanor Roosevelt, or just the president?"

Why did Jon do this? What's holding him back from starting an assignment that should be easy for him to complete?

Jon is a *Confidence-Building Teen*.

What does that mean?

Simply put, he does not yet see himself as separate from his parents, and he's anxious to please them and other authority figures; consequently, he ignores his own intuitions and creative abilities.

He has serious difficulty with self-confidence.

I have worked with many young people who are stuck in the same pattern. Jon was not asking these endless questions because he was lazy or trying to shirk the assignment. He was asking them because he *truly and deeply cared* about the "right" answers.

Jon really wanted to know the exact type of paper that would be acceptable. He cared so much that it had become a source of anxiety that nearly choked off his natural motivation and initiative. He desperately wanted to avoid making mistakes and disappointing his parents.

Jon, like so many good-natured young people I have worked with over the years, was anxious and depressed about his poor school performance. He carefully hid his feelings from his parents and teachers as best he could.

The Confidence-Building Teen rarely experiences happiness because he's too focused on the future, too worried about his performance, or too regretful about the passing of the time when his parents took almost complete care of him.

He may feel responsible for his parents' happiness and therefore represses his own feelings. Consequently, he comes to associate pain and discomfort with doing the right thing. He may exercise, even though he hates it, only because it must be good for him.

His view is, "If it's good for you, it's gotta hurt, right?"

He may exercise out of duty or to please you, but may never develop a love for a sporting activity just because he likes it. For example, a Confidence-Building girl I worked with pursued acting lessons for years because she knew her mom loved the idea of her becoming an actress. She confided to me that she both loved and hated going every week to the lessons. She was deeply ambivalent, but continued going because she imagined her mom would be heartbroken if she stopped. The same can be true for music lessons, clubs, and other activities.

Younger teens may more commonly be building confidence, but older teens may also experience the same approval-seeking tendencies because it may become a long-term personality trait. Many elementary school–aged students who start as approval seekers continue to be into middle and high school. Indeed, many adults are "people-pleasers." Sometimes, conditions in the family may contribute to the "people-pleaser" (also known as the "approval-seeker") orientation.

Where It May Come From

I have worked with many young people who are stuck in the same pattern. A Confidence-Building Teen like Jon really wants to know exactly what behavior would be acceptable in any given situation. He is so focused on pleasing his parents or his teachers that he cannot focus on his own inner voice to answer these questions for himself.

In many families, it's easy for a kid to believe that parents are overly harsh or critical. And kids then have a choice on how to react to this perception—real or imagined.

I recall one such situation with Michael, one of the most intelligent young people I have ever worked with. Without the intention of doing so, Michael's dad, James, contributed to his son's negative perception. James knew how smart he was and hated to see him waste his abilities. He told me that one afternoon he saw Michael totally absorbed in playing a video game and went over to encourage him to go and read, instead of wasting so much time playing the game. Michael skulked away, but did not read. He went to his room and shut the door. Michael later told me that this was just another example of his dad being critical ("I can never do anything right").

Privately, I asked James to tell me what flashed through his mind as he approached Michael. I helped him to reflect a moment and to recall if the situation reminded him of anything that occurred between him and his own father in his childhood. James was able to recall an incident in which he was playing in the backyard with his baseball and pitch-back device by himself. He remembered being totally absorbed in playing each ground ball, pretending he was a major league ball player. His father came over and told him harshly to stop playing and to rake the leaves if he was going to be out in the yard.

With this recollection, James realized that he had essentially repeated the same scenario with Michael. He remembered how dejected he felt as a kid when his dad did not play ball with him but instead lectured him about not doing enough yard work.

A fair amount of the time, when we dig into the teenager's family life, we see conditions that may contribute to the behavior. Michael had begun to see his parents as overly harsh and critical. His father, James, came to the conclusion that he had acted out his jealousy at his son's ability to immerse himself in a fun activity—something he was never allowed to do. Without even realizing it, James was becoming a detriment to his son's growing self-confidence.

In general, this sort of situation may reflect a parent's history of living up to somebody else's prescriptions for success: "Work hard, obey rules, and don't question authority."

Some parents realize their child may not be having as much fun as they would like. Yet to them, success for their kid equates to getting good grades in school. When James saw Michael enjoying a video game, he thought, "This is frivolous. It's not going to help him get ahead in school." So, he became annoyed with Michael and told him to do something "useful." However, James realized upon reflection that all the activities he suggested for Michael were educational in some way. He felt Michael's stress but didn't know what to do about it. Even Michael's mom, Tina, felt their family life had become filled with tension and was not as fun as when Michael was younger. Michael was frustrated that he couldn't please his dad, no matter what he did. He felt like he had two choices: give up trying to please his dad or focus on following all of his father's specific instructions.

I asked James and Tina if there was some way to break this pattern of tense communication between themselves and Michael—especially around homework. James and Tina decided every Saturday would be a purely fun day. No homework allowed. Each member of the family took turns planning a fun activity. Over time, James realized he looked forward to Saturdays as his favorite day of the week. He realized the more fun the family had together, the more Michael did his homework on his own without being reminded. James and Michael even started to carve out a short, fun outing during the week like going to 7-Eleven for a Slurpee together or playing soccer together in the backyard. James and Tina had less conflict regarding parenting Michael and found there was much less tension in their marriage relationship, as well.

The Student's Response

In response to the family environment—and other factors as well—the Confidence-Building Teen may become anxious, angry, or upset, but will hold the feelings inside and become unable to express them.

He may go out to rake the leaves, do his homework, or do whatever else he's been told to do, and become resentful. He internalizes these feelings and becomes understandably depressed or anxious. Frustration grows until he stops doing his schoolwork and chores without specific and direct instruction.

If Michael were to be assertive and tell his father that he would do his homework after completing the level on his video game, he would learn to express the anger and come to understand that his father's issue is not his issue. More open communication would follow.

Once James let go of attempting to manage Michael's time, he felt better knowing Michael was learning to time-manage his homework, chores, and leisure activities. Letting go was tough at first. He realized his pattern of being critical and attempting to dictate Michael's use of his time was not effective.

You may recognize the dynamics of codependency here. Letting go of the part of the problem you cannot control anyway is a good idea. It's invariably part of the solution. And your teen will be free to take action that is his or her own idea. Not yours.

All too often, the Confidence-Building Teen can't bring himself to assertively express his anger or frustration with his parents. Like all Confidence-Building Teens, he had learned not to express his feelings directly. Often, these youths come from a family of high achievers and believe they can't "measure up." But instead of communicating his feelings, he bottles them up, allowing the sense of inadequacy to build.

The Confidence-Building Teen who does poorly in academics is rejecting the expectations of authorities who have always stressed the importance of working hard and obeying all the rules. If she is afraid of overtly telling her parent what she thinks of those expectations, she may end up expressing the anger indirectly by underperforming in school.

Since the Confidence-Building Teen's efforts have always been aimed at pleasing others, he has difficulty deriving any satisfaction from schoolwork, and his frustration grows until he stops doing the work. He may get stuck in the pattern of emphasizing grades rather than enjoying the process of learning something new.

My Family's Experience

I shared with James and Tina some of my family's experiences supporting our son, Alex. We found that our own family had to make some major changes to address Alex's needs.

Shelley, and I noticed that Alex was difficult to understand at times as he learned to talk. When he was three years old, we brought him to a speech-language pathologist for an assessment. Her report was a shock to us. She said he had a severe stuttering problem and that it was so significant that he would probably have this problem for the rest of his life. The assessment also revealed a number of other language acquisition problems. His understanding of vowel sounds was very severely delayed. But the most disturbing news of all was the possible root of the stuttering issue: anxiety. How could our son be overly anxious at the age of three? I couldn't help thinking that, somehow, it must be my fault.

We decided to place Alex immediately in weekly speech-language therapy, but not with the therapist who had made such pessimistic predictions of his future success. We found another SLP (speech-language pathologist) who had a more optimistic outlook. Simply put, there are different schools of thought regarding how to treat stuttering. We wanted to find someone who could support Alex in the best way possible. The SLP we worked with subscribed to an entirely different school of thought from the first that we consulted, using therapeutic techniques to help the child feel *less self-conscious* about stuttering. These techniques included listening patiently, setting aside time to talk, and deliberately NOT correcting the stuttering so as to reduce the overall anxiety.

The new SLP recommended a number of approaches which we did our best to implement. Alex's older sister (age five) would sometimes "interpret" for him, but instead, the SLP suggested that we gently redirect Alex to speak and listen to him in an unhurried and relaxed manner. She suggested an overall reduction in tension in approaching communication (something I dubbed the "Mr. Rogers" approach, named after the famous "laid back" host of the children's television show *Mister Rogers' Neighborhood*; but more about that later).

At the end of two years of therapy, Alex's stuttering was much improved, but his other language acquisition issues remained, which affected his self-confidence, overall anxiety regarding school, and his academic performance. As Alex got older, he developed significant traits of a Confidence-Building Teen as a direct consequence of his learning challenges.

Most of my early memories from childhood come from spending time with speech language pathologists. From my side, I was speaking clearly and felt like I could communicate just fine. The problem was that what came out of my mouth was different from the words I thought I was speaking.

When I was five years old, I went to the bathroom outside my classroom by myself and went to walk back inside. I wasn't sure how to find my way back to the room, so I asked an adult. He said, "Can't you read?" and pointed to the sign. I remember feeling anxious in this moment. It wasn't just because I was being put on the spot. I could hardly speak, and the adult looked at me like I was crazy. This memory has such an impact on me because of the interaction. I could hardly speak, let alone read. I remember his face of shock as I mumbled out what he heard as gibberish. I'm sure he had no idea what was happening and he probably wasn't as abrasive as I remember. But from my perspective, he was such a giant compared to me.

There were other times as a teen when I could feel myself regressing back to stuttering. Stuttering is hard to remember, because I was unaware of my speech. In fact, growing up, I never listened to my own voice. I had no idea what my voice sounded like. But I was quite aware there was a certain amount of time I had to reply to someone before I (and the person listening) felt it was taking too long. This was a lot of pressure. I was trying to funnel the words out within that amount of time. I noticed I would regress if I had a thought I wanted to communicate, but didn't feel that confident in it. It would sound more like a combination of muttering and stuttering.

When I was a teen, we would visit my grandma and grandpa at Lake Tahoe. I explained to her about how I was having trouble making friends that summer. I was worried and not feeling good about making friends; this was something I was very embarrassed about at the time. She gently pointed out, "Alex, sometimes you do mumble and stutter." I was unaware I was actually stuttering until she said this. I remember having to intentionally pull some confidence from myself. I spoke more slowly and more confidently when I explained myself again.

It's interesting being at a different place now and looking back at these issues. I had no idea I was in speech therapy for stuttering. I remember many sessions with several different speech pathologists. Most of the time, I was given a game to play or do some other activity. I didn't really realize how the exercises applied to my everyday life. It was hard to make the connection.

Alex continued in speech therapy and made good progress. Today, I'm very happy to say, he has been able to speak without fluency issues in one-on-one conversation, and he is an excellent public speaker as well.

Generalized Anxiety

If a Confidence-Building Teen has multiple tasks on a particular day, he may feel pressured to schedule them as closely to one another as he can in order not to "waste time" or to get them over with. In contrast, a peer with better time management skills may leave sufficient time between tasks so that he can proceed more leisurely.

The Confidence-Building Teen hurts his performance in school by trying too hard. He'll do one physics experiment five times until everything works out perfectly, but he's so exhausted after this effort that he can't bring himself to do any more complex experiments for the rest of the semester. He may become filled with anxiety during examinations or when giving oral reports. He believes his adequacy and self-worth are based primarily on his performance and his teacher's or peers' approval. He may begin to obsess about an oral presentation until he can't think of anything else. He forgets all the material he knew because of the performance anxiety.

He works hard on the first major assignment for the year. That first assignment is often one of the best in the class. However, he may avoid the intense effort for the rest of the semester. The perfectionism becomes a type of paralysis ("paralysis by analysis"). In the beginning of the semester, he may give up activities he likes in favor of schoolwork. Later in the school year, he procrastinates and avoids his work.

Creativity is stifled by his fear of guessing and new approaches. The Confidence-Building Teen is often so painstaking in his efforts that he doesn't make those intuitive connections that add up to original thinking.

Social Anxiety

Social anxiety is a major problem for the Confidence-Building Teen. She may be described as shy and anxious with peers. Since she wants to be liked, she tries to figure out what interests everyone else. The social anxiety is often overwhelming. She ends up afraid that if she says something positive about a movie, her peers may say they hate that movie. Therefore, she says nothing. The other students don't relate to her because they think she's self-absorbed, a snob, or boring. She may be more subject to peer pressure as a result.

The Confidence-Building Teen will not generally act on reasonable impulses without considering the reaction of others. If she wants to go to an animated movie, she may think peers will find the movie "stupid" or "for little kids." She always takes external "shoulds" into account when making decisions.

Some Confidence-Building Teens can be highly competitive because their self-esteem depends largely upon how well they do compared to other people, but generally they are afraid to do well. They may worry about being labeled "a teacher's pet."

Performance Anxiety

Forcing a Confidence-Building Teen to speak in a group discussion when they are anxious to do so is not recommended. They will gradually begin to speak more frequently in the group without prodding as they experience positive feelings and see peers learn to talk in the group.

A Connection Response can be used with the quiet student in the context of a group discussion: "It's hard for you to say the things you want to say, but I have the feeling there are things you'd like to share" or "I would like to hear your thoughts." Then, turn back and continue with the group discussion.

Such Connection Responses will encourage the student to focus on what they would like to say instead of seeking the approval of the group.

If your teen seems to be uncomfortable with a particular topic, don't put him or her on the spot. The Confidence-Building Teen's anxiety will shoot through the roof and he or she will clam up, perhaps for many weeks afterward. The teacher should not publicly, directly point out the anxiety by saying, "What's wrong? You seem to be uptight."

This type of remark tends to embarrass the student. It is much more effective to be reassuring with a supportive Connection Response: "You seem to be feeling a little uncomfortable with what we are talking about . . ." and then move on with the discussion, shifting the attention away from the teen.

The student who is anxious about making a class presentation or speech may also be unsure of how to relate to peers. The source of the anxiety is the possible embarrassment in front of peers, rather than the possibility of receiving a poor grade.

I consulted with a teacher, Ms. Ross, who wanted to supportively encourage a student, Garrett, to share his feelings about the presentation. She told me Garrett outright refused to make the oral presentation: "I can't make that speech."

I recommended possible Connection Responses. She recounted a couple of the conversations she had with Garrett.

Ms. Ross: "It's really important to you to do your absolute best, isn't it, Garrett?"

Garrett: "I just get so nervous when I speak in front of the group."

Ms. Ross: "You really want others to like you. I understand, and it's natural to feel a bit anxious before speaking in front of a group. It can be scary when you are not sure what others may be thinking of you."

This approach is much more effective than a response like, "Everything will be fine," "Just dive in!" or "Don't worry; I always get nervous when I make speeches, too." These responses tend to focus on the teacher rather than the student's feelings.

My Family's Experience

When he reached fifth grade, Alex became so anxious about his school performance he began to hide his homework because he was concerned he could not complete it correctly. Shelley had spent at least a half hour with him every night reading with him since he was in kindergarten. Sometimes, they were both really tired at the end of the day, yet Shelley prioritized the individual time with him every evening reading an enjoyable age-appropriate book. Alex, for his part, was already a perceptive and empathic person. He would try to get out of the reading session by suggesting, "Mom, if you're tired we don't have to read tonight . . ." Shelley always gently thanked him, but still spent the time reading with him.

I am one of the luckiest people on earth to have a mom who was so patient with me. I have a memory of reading a book about a slumber party when I was just beginning to read. It took me and my mom a half hour to finish just one page and the entire week to read the book. It wasn't until I was older that I realized the book had only two sentences per page. My mom patiently encouraged me to make the individual sound for each letter and then put it all together. She would then go back to the beginning of the sentence and have me put everything together. If she hadn't put in the time with me, I would have never learned to read.

I started to memorize words and that helped my reading fluency. I got to the point where I could read most of the sentences, but I would always have at least one word I would have to sound out.

I have a distinct memory of me begging my mom not to read one night. I questioned the importance of reading, and my mom responded by saying, "Alex, one day you'll thank me for doing this." I remember being so shocked by her response because there was no way I could see how this was going to be important. But I believed her, and I began reading our book.

By the time I reached middle school, I remember being embarrassed about still reading aloud with my mom. I still enjoyed most of the stories we would read. I remember To Kill a Mocking Bird *quite well. I also remember reading*

Around the World in Eighty Days. After I "silent read" the book, the teacher decided to read the book out loud to the class. I could remember finally piecing the sentences together as she read; however, I had no idea what the story was actually about until I heard it out loud.

I did not enjoy recreational reading until much later in life. I actually enjoyed reading manuals more when I was younger because they were short and very informative. They were easy to understand and taught me useful information, compared to stories that had so many moving parts. Even today, I'm not a big fan of fiction books. I just don't get the same enjoyment out of them as I do more educational or nonfiction material. It was really hard for me to develop a larger picture of the text. I would be focused on the details and miss what the sentences were actually saying about the entire story.

The Effect of Anxiety

The Confidence-Building Teen's personality causes him anxiety at school due to indecisiveness. He tends to feel torn between expectations of different authority figures.

If the teacher tells the class to do an opinion paper on any subject, the Confidence-Building Teen experiences anxiety and considers each topic on the long list of possibilities before reaching a decision. He may guess at what topic the teacher wants him to select. Even then he has to figure out which side of the issue to take. Fear of making a wrong decision paralyzes him.

Indecisiveness also affects the Confidence-Building Teen during class discussions. When the teacher asks a question, he tends to obsessively focus on the numerous reasons for being on either side of the issue.

Warning Signs

Usually, parents need not be concerned about self-destructive or antisocial tendencies, because Confidence-Building Teens already have inhibitions against such behavior.

However, many experts have noted that more teens than ever are suffering from full-blown anxiety disorders.[1] These kids have become so depressed and anxious that they may have already had some thoughts of self-harm because it feels like there is no way to meet the expectations that have been placed upon them. They feel there is no way out. Some students may not want to attend school and refuse to go.

Others may be picked on by cyberbullies or bullies at the school. It is important for parents to investigate school situations that involve bullying and get the school administration involved.

It is of the utmost importance that parents seek professional counseling with a teen that has become so depressed that thoughts of self-harm or suicide are present. Open communication and "checking in" with your teen are also vitally important. Be available when she wants to talk (which may not be a convenient time for you). Gently ask, "How are you today?" and be open to a lengthily response or a short "fine" depending on her mood. Use Connection Responses. Be open to professional counseling to help support yourself and your teen.

Goals and Milestones

The primary goal with the Confidence-Building Teen is to help them to experience and express emotions. It is equally important that they begin to separate their own desires from the desires and expectations of others. As they gain confidence, they will learn to act spontaneously and others will respond favorably.

As the Confidence-Building Teen learns more about their feelings and intuitive desires, they open their thought process more readily and become more creative in their thinking.

The Confidence-Building Teen may not look at problems in new and unusual ways. As they become less anxious, they no longer attempt rigid control over emotions and become less perfectionistic. Many teens who are in the process of learning to be more comfortable with themselves accept their own personal best instead of trying to reach perfection.

The key to helping the Confidence-Building Teen, then, is to assist them in expressing feelings more fully. This is why the Connection Response—which reflects back feelings—is so important.

Effective Communication

I have observed that effective communication with the Confidence-Building Teen really starts with establishing the right kind of relationship. He must feel comfortable sharing feelings and reactions without fear of punishment or criticism. Parents' and teachers' body language and voice level are most effective when they are low-key and as non-judgmental as possible. This will help the student to concentrate on himself and how he is feeling.

If parents are too overpowering, they tend to make him more aware of *their* thoughts and feelings. In response, he becomes more anxious and will start trying to please the parents instead of himself.

I was able to point out to James that his strong opinion about how Michael's interest in video gaming was a waste of time had backfired. Michael thought only of how his dad was displeased and disapproving of him. Michael had lost his sense of himself in the conflict.

Remember that the Confidence-Building Teen is not very good at discerning his own thoughts and feelings. Communicating with him requires a degree of patience and gentleness that may not come naturally to most parents.

I call it being "Mr. or Mrs. Rogers" of *Mister Rogers' Neighborhood* fame. Kids were captivated by Fred Rogers's gentle and quiet demeanor. He represented a quiet, gentle, and calming figure in their lives. The Confidence-Building Teen responds best to the Mr. Rogers in all of us. A gentle, encouraging approach can work wonders in encouraging self-awareness and self-expression.

The Confidence-Building Teen may benefit from a quiet environment where parents don't ask too many questions, but rather allow the teen to initiate conversation. This is the beginning of healing, connection, and better engagement.

Non-Verbal Communication

Effective communication with the Confidence-Building Teen really starts with establishing the right kind of relationship. Modeling, or setting a positive example, is the most powerful of your communication tools. Really take the time to focus when you speak with them. Your non-verbal behaviors—posture, facial expression, movements, and physical closeness—all matter very much to the way you come across. Voice tone matters a lot, too.

If you are preoccupied with thoughts about work, tasks, or other things on your plate, your son or daughter will undoubtedly pick up on it. And your communication will suffer.

I reviewed the importance of Relatedness, Autonomy, and Competence in the family environment with James. I explained the research on how these elements help teens to develop the essential, non-cognitive quality of intrinsic motivation. James discussed the matter with Tina and made a rather profound change in the way he related to Michael. The next time he saw Michael playing his video game, he chose to sit down next to him. He showed some interest in the game, and refrained from asking about his homework or making comments about the best use of his time. After reflecting about the issue, he realized this was one among many ways he could contribute to developing Relatedness in their family environment.

My Family's Experience

Our SLP recommended we take one-on-one time with Alex each and every day to be with him alone, just fifteen or twenty minutes each day of uninterrupted time (we called it "Individual Time"). We decided our other kids should also get Individual Time. As a result, our whole family benefitted. We continued the tradition for many years, even after Alex's formal therapy with the SLP had finished and he had begun school-based speech-language therapy.

Individual Time meant no distractions. No radio, television, or internet. No electronics. Playing a video game or watching TV together didn't count. Playing a board game or putting together a puzzle was OK. Throwing a ball in the yard was great. Any activity where we had direct interaction worked. Our SLP emphasized *non-demand* interaction was key. So there was no insistence on eye contact, "useful" communication, or any other demand whatsoever really. We just enjoyed pure uninterrupted relaxed time together.

I don't directly remember any of the Individual Time because it was integrated into my typical schedule. I remember going on outings with my dad. He would take me for ice cream, and he would also take special time with me every night. We did shadow puppets before bedtime and prayed together. I have a lot of truly wonderful memories with my dad. This was a part of the day where I felt like I could ask my dad anything. I always loved the amount of time he would spend with me.

I also don't really remember a heavy use of internet or electronics. I valued my individual time with my parents a lot. I also remember playing made up games with my sister in our yard more than video games. We always had fun exploring and playing together. I got lucky that video games were not around and I had my family to play with.

It was also my mom's rule that each of us had to play a sport. I played baseball in middle school and moved on to other sports afterward. My mom also had the idea that she wanted us to try a lot of different sports. She bought me a surfboard as a present with a surfing lesson. I still surf today. I saw that my parents' emphasis on activities like sports helped my whole family—myself most of all—develop confidence. And it was fun.

The Connection Response

A very helpful response that we use with the Confidence-Building Teen is the *Connection Response*. Recall, it both acknowledges the feeling that underlies words and encourages the connection of other situations when he may have felt the same way. The Connection Response may start with simply restating your teen's feelings ("Looks like that made you feel [mad, sad, glad, upset, disappointed, excited, etc.]"). In doing this, you seek to clarify the feeling content *and* encourage more insight.

The second part is important as well. You may offer your educated guess to coax further self-discovery ("So, not only did you feel mad about it, but the whole thing reminded you about what [your friend, girlfriend, teacher] said before that made you mad before"). The Connection Response includes your connection with your teen and—at the same time—their connection to their own feelings and insights. Your teen may accept or reject your educated guesses about their feelings and insights. It's even better if you were incorrect and your teen corrects you and clarifies by telling you, "No, I felt more [sad, rejected, etc.] than angry." The Connection Response helps your teen to acknowledge the feelings that underlie their words and encourages them to think of other situations in which they felt the same way. As we have discussed, being a good listener means focusing attention on your teen and refraining from formulating an answer before they have finished speaking. Teens are especially good at detecting whether a parent or teacher is really listening or is simply waiting to continue talking (or lecturing).

As a parent, you can be a model for becoming a good listener. In most situations, modeling is the most powerful way to teach non-cognitive skills. As Gandhi said, "Be the change you wish to see." As a parent, you can listen, pick out highlights of a conversation, and make good Connection Responses in return. It helps to model listening by looking your teen in the eye and turning off the television or putting the smartphone down to make sure there is no distraction by outside interference—all aspects of non-verbal communication that we've previously discussed.

Sarah and Her Mother, Stephanie

In my work with families, I find a lot of obstacles to communication. Sarah, a smart and sensitive young woman, told me, "My mother never understands anything I say." Really, she was frustrated at her inability to express herself to others in general, but she believed that her mother was responsible for the lack of communication between them.

I recommended Connection Responses to her mother, Stephanie. We had to drill down to the core reasons the connection between them had broken in the first place.

Stephanie described the typical conversation she had with Sarah ("Sarah comes home from school. I ask her how her day went. She says 'OK.' I ask her if she had any new assignments I can help her with. She says 'no.' If I ask anything else, I get one-word answers").

My assignment for Stephanie was to avoid asking too many questions. I assigned her to ask only open-ended questions or to make Connection Responses. We rehearsed the kind of things she might say to Sarah. If Sarah came home looking gloomy, I suggested she might say, "Looks like it was a tough day . . ." If Sarah came home looking happy, I suggested she could say something like, "Must have been a good day. You look bright and cheerful!"

I told Stephanie that, at first, Sarah would probably say nothing or grunt one-word answers as usual. I urged her to patiently wait and say nothing more than Connection Responses or very open-ended questions ("Is there anything you want to talk about?").

A week later, Stephanie told me what happened: "You were right. For the first few days, Sarah just said 'yeah' in response to my Connection Responses. But the fourth day, she volunteered a little more about what happened at school that day. I resisted the temptation to comment on what she told me or to ask questions. I stuck with pure Connection Responses as you suggested. She told me her friends were kinda mean to her that day. I don't approve of these so-called friends. I think she is hanging with the wrong crowd. But instead of commenting, I listened and said, 'That must have made you feel sad.'

She agreed and told me a bit more about what they said to her."

For Stephanie, this was a near-miraculous outcome. Sarah hadn't confided in her in this way for a very long time. She was enthusiastic about using Connection Responses with Sarah, even though she still found it difficult to resist the temptation to ask multiple questions to pry more information out of Sarah about how things were going with her friends and at school.

These days, I often see smartphones, television, video, and other electronic distractions keep families from communicating clearly with one another. Confidence-Building Teens benefit from parents making an effort to use Connection Responses. A typical response could be, "I can see it's hard for you to tell other people how you really feel about things, especially when they don't look like they are listening because of an iPhone in their hand" (make sure to put down your smartphone when you say this!). Notice the response is not an excuse. It places the responsibility for clear communication on the young person, yet also acknowledges his or her feelings ("It's hard for you . . . yet it is important for you to do it").

Using the Connection Response

Effectively using the Connection Response requires that we listen closely for the feeling that the person is describing. The next step is to let her know that you understand her emotion by describing it without mentioning the particular present issue.

When the Confidence-Building Teen hears the Connection Response, she may think to herself, "Yes, I have felt like that before," and she will go on to remember and describe other experiences in which she had the same feeling. Each time such a situation arises, you may use other Connection Responses to give her opportunity to experience and/or share more of her feelings.

In time, she will become familiar enough with the process of introspection that she learns to process her own feelings more readily.

The Confidence-Building Teen will eventually gain insight into her feelings of powerlessness and stop associating these feelings with the momentary anger against her mother. Eventually, she will discover that her fear of others' disapproval is rooted in the fact that she does not tell others what she wants.

The impact of effective communication with the Confidence-Building Teen is different for each individual. Some teens and young adults seem to become less anxious or depressed almost immediately. Within a few weeks, they are sharing their feelings much more readily. Others take longer because they have internalized more feelings.

Parents and teachers may find that they require an entire semester and hundreds of Connection Responses before there is a significant move toward independence.

In learning how to make Connection Responses, parents and teachers may find it helpful to write down as many typical statements made by the Confidence-Building Teen as they can remember. Practice making a Connection Response is as important as listening with an open mind.

The more accustomed we become with using Connection Responses, the better we are at choosing an appropriate one for a particular conversation.

Common Situations

Particular situations come up repeatedly with the Confidence-Building Teen, and it is helpful to examine how specific responses may be applied.

Deep down, the Confidence-Building Teen wishes that they could learn to do activities they enjoy instead of pleasing their parents. To help them become aware of this desire, we can use Connection Responses.

In my work with Jon, whom you may recall from the beginning of this chapter, I used many Connection Responses to help him get in touch with his feelings. For example, he would sometimes complain about school in general terms. I would respond with an educated guess by reflecting the possible source of his feelings ("You're so sick and tired of everyone's expectations you feel like you simply can't take it anymore"). I would also sometimes use selective self-disclosure to encourage some insight: "You seem overwhelmed. I know I sometimes feel that way when I get tired of everyone else's expectations of me. That's when I take some alone time and use that self-relaxation and Mindful Meditation stuff we talked about. I call it my 'five-minute vacation.'"

"It feels good not to do everything that you're expected to do sometimes."

"I see you can't wait for the day when you can run your own life. That seems so far away."

Kyle and His Stepmom, Rhonda

Kyle is a thirteen-year-old Confidence-Building Teen, and Rhonda is his stepmom.

Here's how one of their conversations went as reported by Rhonda.

> Rhonda: "Kyle, you look like you are frustrated this afternoon."
>
> Kyle: "Every time I play a video game, I feel bad about playing. I know I should get my homework done."
>
> Rhonda: "You feel bad because you know there's homework to be done."
>
> Kyle: "Yeah. Maybe I need to do a half hour of homework before I play and finish the rest later."
>
> Rhonda: "Getting a little done before playing can help. I often feel like that, too."

Sometimes, waiting with the Confidence-Building Teen silently and just being present is a way to show encouragement and support. At other times, waiting expectantly for him to clarify or follow up is helpful. Sometimes, it's better to make a Connection Response and be silent or even walk away.

Notice Rhonda threw in a bit of self-disclosure ("I often feel like that, too"). Sometimes, sharing your experience as a kid or even sharing recent experiences can build a powerful connection with your teen. I am not suggesting a parent "lean on" their teen or get extensive support. As a parent, you are there to *provide* support. However, selective and considered self-disclosure can be a way to build empathy and give the important encouragement your teen needs at just the right moment.

Sometimes, it may appear that the Confidence-Building Teen hasn't heard the Connection Response. However, there is no need to repeat the comment. He may return sometime in the next several days and talk about other thoughts that have been triggered by Connection Responses.

In this way, parents will realize that the connection is having an effect. If parents wait expectantly for concrete signs of progress, too often the young person will detect the attitude and avoid further communication.

Instead, use Connection Responses as a regular way to communicate. Let go of the power struggle. Respond and let go.

It is also important to help the teen to develop assertiveness skills and start to express feelings more readily.

Assertiveness Skills

Assertiveness is defined as simply stating what you need or what you want. The difference between *assertiveness and aggressiveness* is that you are stating your needs and wants without attacking or putting down the other person. Modeling assertiveness is an important feature of influencing your teen's skill set. As such, assertiveness has to do with communicating effectively with others.

How can you model assertiveness effectively? It requires being direct about what you need and want while acknowledging the needs and wants of others. When you are assertive, you ask for what you want while knowing that you may not get it. It is not *demanding what you want. It is asking* for what you want directly in straightforward language.

Kids model the behavior of their parents. When your teen sees that you are being assertive—rather than aggressive or passive—with other family members, they will be more likely to learn this skill. Assertive statements are generally "I" statements or "I feel" statements. Practice using "I" statements and "I feel" statements in your communication with all family members.

Often, a conflict escalates when parents use "You" statements instead of "I" statements. These statements often promote blaming the other person. For example, if the statement is "You are making me sad," then an "I" statement might be "I feel sad when you don't hug me."

In making an "I" statement, avoid using "You" statements imbedded inside the "I" statement. For example, "I think you are being a jerk!" is not an effective "I" statement. A more effective way to express anger might be "I feel angry when you talk that way" or, even better, "I feel angry when you cuss at me."

The word "you" can be used in part of the statement so that it is not a blaming statement. If there is something the person does that really does upset you, describe the behavior you can see.

In the example above, "when you cuss at me" is more descriptive than if you say, "when you talk that way." Another example of a "You" statement is "You better get out of here!" An "I" statement that could be used instead would be, "I really need some space now."

Sometimes, it's not easy to be assertive as a teen or young adult, especially with peers. For example, your teen may experience a situation in which a friend has been drinking, but the friend insists he's OK to drive home. Your child senses danger, but doesn't know what to say.

As a parent, you can bring up the topic—perhaps after seeing a movie or television show with a similar situation—and suggest possible responses. Brainstorm with your teen to see what would feel natural or easy to say. Maybe something like, "I know how much you've had to drink, and I don't think you're OK to drive. We're friends, and our friendship is important to me, but I don't feel right getting in the car with you right now."

Using Connection Responses to Encourage Assertiveness

The Confidence-Building Teen may attempt to get the teacher to rescue him from the anxiety of relating to peers. I consulted with a teacher, Ms. Tyler, who told me that her student Miguel complained, "Hey, Carlos keeps talking to me. Tell him to stop!" Miguel asked Ms. Tyler to put his desk in the front of the class to keep Carlos from distracting him.

What Miguel was really asking was for Ms. Tyler to take care of his peer issues. I advised her it was better to allow Miguel to work out the issue himself.

I brainstormed some possible Connection Responses to encourage assertiveness: "Miguel, it can be difficult for you to get others to understand what you want," and "Standing up for yourself can be difficult sometimes."

Ms. Tyler was also able to facilitate clear communication between Carlos and Miguel. She modeled assertive statements like, "Carlos, I want you to focus on your work."

Encouraging Social Skills

Many Confidence-Building Teens have difficulty relating to others. In social situations, they may feel anxious because they fear they are saying the "wrong thing" and peers won't like them. The anxiety actually causes their minds to go blank and contributes to the social awkwardness. They worry that they may come across socially as boring, self-absorbed, or unintelligent.

Social media like Facebook, Instagram, Snapchat, and others can increase social anxiety in a number of ways.[2] Teens respond to texts, post to Facebook, follow others' seemingly perfect lives on their "timeline" or "feed," and worry their lives just can't measure up.

Some say that teens with social anxiety are excessively self-conscious. Yes, but in addition, shy teens are also intensely "other-conscious" in the sense that they worry very much about how others will think of them.[3]

To spare themselves anxiety, they may carefully speak and organize their thoughts, losing all spontaneity, or isolate themselves with internet social contact instead of seeing peers in live social situations.

Parents can help Confidence-Building Teens talk more naturally to others by encouraging them to speak freely and move from one topic to another. They will, therefore, respond to what the other person says they're feeling, rather than trying to be clever or interesting.

Some teens who want to have a special relationship with their teachers are unable to relate well with peers. Teens like this may have trouble making friends. Confidence-Building Teens may become seekers of approval who generally relate better to adults than they do to their peers. They feel less anxiety in talking with adults. Often, they have learned to focus on gaining acceptance from authority figures over learning social skills and ways to start conversations with their peers.

When parents notice these tendencies in their child, it can be easy to try to overcompensate. Some parents may use a lot of verbal praise to try to raise their kid's self-esteem.

Allison, a mother who had read several books on parenting, attempted to use excessive praise to raise the low self-esteem of her son, Evan ("You are such a great ball player!"). He told me his friends made fun of him when his mom made some well-meaning comments to him after he played in the baseball game. Evan's self-esteem actually sank lower. He knew he wasn't the best player on the team. The comment unintentionally focused Evan away from his internal feelings and self-awareness and onto his mom's expectations and approval.

Ryan, a thirteen-year-old, showed his mother, Ann, some art that he created in art class. Ann smiled and said, "Ryan, this is wonderful. I'm so proud of you. I knew you were an artist; you get it from me." At least in part, Ann experiences success vicariously through him. She also states her own feeling about the achievement.

Ryan begins to understand that his goal is to make her happy. He has learned to seek approval. Over time, Ryan begins to like art less but felt afraid to tell Ann, because she had invested in art lessons and supplies.

The Connection Response would be something like "Ryan, this is wonderful and you look really happy with it!" The comment would help to remove the focus from Ann's feelings and response and would place the emphasis on Ryan's own internal response to his achievement.

If Ryan seemed unhappy with his work, she could say, "I can see that you're not happy with your artwork." Parents may attempt to lift up a Confidence-Building Teen who expresses disappointment with their own work by saying, "It's OK; you'll do better next time."

Unfortunately, such statements can actually increase the anxiety and sadness the Confidence-Building Teen feels because the listener seems to be dismissing his feelings. The Connection Response ("I can see that you're not happy with your artwork") helps the teen to get in touch with their own feelings. The most reassuring thing for any of us is to know that another person understands how we feel, especially if we are sad or upset.

Parents who believe excessive praise is necessary to motivate their teen may themselves be approval seekers. They may assume that a teen will not be motivated without praise from others. Similarly, parents who believe sharp criticism is necessary to motivate a young person often experienced such criticism in their own childhood and adolescence.

It is far better to help the student feel a sense of fulfillment from inside in response to their achievements. In this way, *intrinsic motivation*—motivation from inside not outside—is nurtured and developed.

Ever notice how high achievers continue to work even when their achievements are notable? Even after achieving fame, fortune, and praise from everyone, many successful people continue to work long hours and are motivated to reach their new goals. I'm not talking about workaholics here, but rather people who are motivated from the inside to reach their goals because they have learned to feel good when they see themselves learning and moving forward each day. Such healthy motivation comes from intrinsic motivation—feeling good about one's accomplishments from the inside.

It is good to give a teen praise for work well done. It is even better to give such praise only after focusing on your teen's own feelings, so the emphasis is on the process rather than the outcome alone ("You feel [surprised, happy, pleased] with how well you did!").

The 100 Percent Responsibility Rule

Managing your Confidence-Building Teen, particularly when they are crossing the line in their behavior, can be a challenge! Determining what your responsibility is, as compared to theirs, can help you find balance and healing connection.

The Confidence-Building Teen may have the exact opposite problem of the teen or young adult who stops trying: no matter how hard they try, they believe they can never meet the performance standards of his teachers and parents. There's always a little bit more they could do.

In desperation, they may turn to cheating on tests and assignments, hoping to get better grades and maintain self-esteem. They may feel parents and other family members are overachievers, and there is no way to compete.

The Confidence-Building Teen inevitably grows unhappy achieving in school simply in response to teachers' and parents' expectations. They feel no sense of fulfillment from academic work. They may be afraid of overtly expressing anger at parents or may indirectly express the anger by underperforming at school. They may also be suffering from anxiety so that the very thought of failure at school paralyzes them when they start to do the work.

The Independence-Building, Initiative-Building, or Identity-Building student who cheats should experience significant consequences and should be carefully monitored to make sure the cheating stops. However, the Confidence-Building Teen should be approached somewhat differently. It is important to make sure the cheating behavior stops; however, it is equally important to place less emphasis on discipline and more emphasis on helping the Confidence-Building Teen understand where their behavior is coming from.

A parent could use the Connection Response, "Sometimes, you feel like no matter how hard you try or what you do, somehow you're still not good enough." This type of response can help him or her become aware of his feelings of extreme frustration. Certainly, when you've addressed their feelings, it is important to establish that it's not OK to cheat or lie. It is also important not to reinforce your teen's sense of inadequacy.

Family counseling can be helpful. The issue of the parents' expectations can be addressed. It is helpful for parents to change their expectations and be less critical overall. Many parents resist the suggestion of family counseling because they believe it's a negative reflection on the family. Rather, it can be an opportunity to help you better understand your current communications and adjust appropriately.

It is natural to want your son or daughter to succeed, but it is also important that they feel ownership of the success. Remember that the grades your child brings home aren't yours! Some young people "push back" as a way to rebel when they sense a parent wants their success more than they do. Moreover, they may begin to perceive all adults as being as intrusive and controlling. This may in turn lead to lying behavior at school as well as at home.

Ignoring the lying behavior can be better than getting into a power struggle. I am not suggesting that parents should ignore serious acting-out behaviors. On the contrary, taking active steps to address the more serious, underlying behavioral issues may be necessary.

In this case, lying behavior is really an attempt to assert identity and independence. It is important to target the underlying behavior rather than the lying behavior itself. Some parents may try to assert more control when their teen is caught in a lie. This, in turn, may lead to even more lying behavior in a vicious cycle.

Instead, use the 100 Percent Responsibility Rule to figure out a reasonable parental response to the behavior. What is your responsibility as a parent in this situation? Take 100 percent responsibility for your part by formulating a well thought out parental response. Take zero percent of your teen's responsibility. Leave that to him. For example, if your teen lied about coming home on time after a night out, it's important to decide what matters in the situation. Was he out with friends and acting responsibly? Did he simply want to stay out later? That situation may be very different from a young person who has been using illegal drugs or hanging out with peers who are likely to get him in trouble. Tailor your response based on the situation rather than the issue of being told a lie.

Like Jon in history class, some Confidence-Building Teens seem unable to follow simple directions, but rather ask a string questions before proceeding to the next step. In answering the questions, teachers and parents may be encouraging him to become even more dependent.

Instead of answering the questions use a connection response, such as "It's hard to figure out what you want to do."

The student may rephrase his questions in several ways. Use a Connection Response each time. It may seem that you are being repetitive, but in reality, you are encouraging him to become aware of his feeling state. Withdrawing attention is also an effective strategy if the young person is persistent with the same question over and over. It is your responsibility to outline the basic assignment and help him with aspects that are beyond his capacity. Anything that your teen can reasonably accomplish on his own is his responsibility.

If the teen begins to connect with his own feelings, he may gain some insight and stop asking the constant questions whose only purpose is to gain reassurance from the teacher or parent. Teens who talk constantly are often Confidence-Building Teens who use their communication mainly as a way to gain attention and reassurance in response to their anxiety.

One could approach the situation using behavior modification by rewarding the student for remaining quiet for a certain period of time. However, this strategy could lead to a power struggle. The use of a connection response is a more effective tactic. In a relaxed tone of voice, one could observe "Maybe you're having a rough day today," or "It seems you're feeling a bit anxious or upset today."

Encouraging your teen to think about other situations in his life that are upsetting can help them to become aware of feelings about these issues. Consequently, they may begin to self-disclose about the issues and feelings about them ("I hate it when teachers don't give an outline for the assignment").

Confidence-Building Teens may become overly attached to teachers and may actively seek the teacher's approval in various situations to gain acceptance and praise. The teacher who actively seeks "teacher's pets" may be an approval-seeking personality herself. She may be gaining positive feelings by granting special privileges in return for the student's admiration and esteem. It is important for teachers to avoid making particular students favorites, since these relationships tend to reinforce the student's dependence on the teacher. It may also adversely affect the student's relationship with peers. Unfortunately, these codependent relationships don't follow the 100 Percent Responsibility Rule. The teachers take on responsibility for their student's confidence and esteem.

Making Progress

As the Confidence-Building Teen becomes aware of his feelings and discloses them to others, watch for signs that he is moving toward independence. The teen may show more energy and appear more alert. As they allow their feelings to surface, they tend to experience a burden lifted from their shoulders and show more spontaneity.

As a Confidence-Building Teen improves, they appear more confident and assertive. They don't worry about what others may think as much as previously. They make eye contact more readily. They no longer have nervous tics that were an expression of anxiety.

With the decrease in anxiety comes an accompanying increase in the teen's ability to form relationships with peers. They are more curious about others and particularly about the issues that matter to them at an emotional level. They may reject friendships with peers who are too conscious of their image or being "cool." Instead, they might gravitate toward someone who is not very popular, yet is unafraid of being a separate, unique individual.

At the same time that the maturing Confidence-Building Teen develops better relationships with his peers, they are willing to strike out on their own if anyone disagrees with them.

Frank hung around with a group that constantly picked on a vulnerable student, Leo, in the class. He told me he was afraid to say anything about it because he might end up being picked on, too. As Frank felt more confident in himself, he became aware of how upset he felt when his friends said mean things to Leo. He took a risk and said, "Man, that's just not cool" once when he thought they had gone too far.

It takes a strong individual—an individual who knows his own intuitions and acts on them—to risk friendship in this way. The changing Confidence-Building Teen will also demonstrate more confidence and assertiveness.

Ms. Tyler observed a student in her classroom named Elena. She volunteered more frequently and even ventured answers to questions that she was not absolutely sure about, because her self-esteem no longer depended on always being right. She disagreed with other students or with the teacher at times. She confidently rephrased her statement in a group discussion if someone asked her what she meant.

You may also see more creativity in written work because the progressing Confidence-Building Teen now feels free to experiment and to express things that really matter to them emotionally. Whereas before they approached every assignment in a rational, logical manner, now they have opened up to intuition and make highly creative connections.

For the same reason, they are more creative and the Confidence-Building Teen no longer fears evaluative situations. Expressing thoughts and feelings honestly is more important than being right. They do not feel their self-esteem is on the line whenever they take a test or write a paper. In fact, because of the more relaxed attitude, they often do better in school than when they fretted over every grade.

Perhaps the most significant change in the Confidence-Building Teen will occur in relationships with parents and teachers. Toward both parents and teachers, they begin to assert themselves, state disagreements, and truly develop the qualities of confidence and initiative.

In fact, sometimes, the teen may seem to speak disrespectfully. As a parent or teacher, don't become too defensive or reprimand the teen for showing signs of independence. Just ignore mildly disrespectful language or, even better, use a Connection Response like, "You really feel strongly about that."

Given time and patience on your part, the Confidence-Building Teen will become much more comfortable with himself and with others. He is in the process of separating his own ideas from the expectations of others he has internalized.

Key Action Steps ✓

- Use Connection Responses frequently to build feelings of Relatedness, Autonomy, and Competence.
- The Confidence-Building Teen needs to be approached in a supportive manner. It is important not to add to their anxiety about performance.
- Teachers and parents should avoid criticism and, instead, be supportive.
- Teach stress management techniques such as relaxation, meditation, slow breathing, mindfulness, and physical activity.
- Approach this type of teen in a gentle way ("You know, I'm worried about bringing this up. You know why? I'm afraid you'll hear it in a negative way as a criticism. But that's not the way I mean it"). This approach will make it much less likely that the teen will become more anxious about trying to achieve.
- Use the 100 Percent Responsibility Rule to strike a balance between assisting your teen and encouraging independence. It is important not to allow the Confidence-Building Teen to become too dependent on others. The general principle is, "Don't do for your teen what they can do for themselves."
- Look into the issues behind the teen's behavior. If this is not possible, seek counseling for the student as a safe place he or she can express feelings.
- Encourage increased physical activity and use of relaxation techniques.
- Discuss negative beliefs and gently challenge false assumptions. Don't give false praise. The Confidence-Building Teen will interpret this in a negative manner. After you give feedback, use a Connection Response to check if they interpreted what you said as it was intended.
- Encourage him to create objectives that are well defined, easily accomplished, and represent small steps toward a larger goal. For

example, help the student to create a simple checklist. Keep it very short with just two or three items. When these items are checked off, the day is declared a success.

- Allow them to make their own homework schedule.
- As a parent, explore how you cope with your own anxiety, procrastination, or moodiness. Is your teen modeling behavior he or she has seen?

CHAPTER 5

The Independence-
Building Teen

Remember Carlos? He is the fifteen-year-old teen with brown hair, brown eyes, and disheveled clothes usually a few sizes too big. He was withdrawn and shy but often short and disrespectful with teachers and his parents. He started hanging out with a "bad crowd" and frequently cut afternoon classes to meet up with his friends. His father drank a lot and his parents argued about the issue of alcohol abuse. He started referring to his father as a "dick" when talking about him. His grades began slid to Ds and Fs when he entered high school.

He locked his mom out of the house for two hours one afternoon and denied doing it. He showed no remorse whatsoever for treating his mother this way. He smirked and pretended the incident never happened. "Maybe she couldn't open the door or something . . ." he said.

Since Carlos often complained about his father's drinking and his parents' fights, I dryly made an observation at the end of one of our counseling sessions after we finished playing chess. I said, "Locking your mother out of the house sounds like a kinda 'dick-like' thing to do." I made sure not to imply any negative or judgmental message. It was merely a neutral statement made with a rather matter-of-fact tone. And this was said only after about two months of weekly counseling sessions during which I listened, largely without comment, to Carlos's complaints about his family.

The very next session I met with Carlos's mother beforehand, as was my custom. She said his behavior had turned around 180 degrees. He was more respectful, even kind and helpful. Moreover, he had begun to do his homework regularly. During my session with Carlos, I never mentioned his turnaround in behavior nor my comment the previous session. I merely made a few open-ended Connection Responses during our usual game of chess. I reflected how he appeared to be feeling that week—rather calm and less tense. He didn't comment on my statement or correct it. We just played chess. Carlos had made the connection between his angry attitude toward his father and his angry behavior toward his mother. He didn't want to become like his dad. I knew it and he knew it. I needn't have made any explicit statements about it. He made the connection and made the changes. I didn't even compliment him. I just let my simple Connection Response stand as a note that I had perceived the change he had made.

Character Strengths and the Independence-Building Teen

Since Character Strengths like grit, self-control, optimism, and conscientiousness are described accurately as non-cognitive skills, teachers and school districts have attempted to develop these traits in their students like skills that we know how to teach: reading, math, logic, etc. As Character Strengths have become more widely regarded as important, many have attempted to develop a curriculum to help students develop the skills. Some schools have developed comprehensive approaches to teaching non-cognitive skills. It's more popular than ever for teachers to talk to their students directly about qualities like perseverance and self-control. In practice, however, a paradox is quite noticeable; many of the teachers who seem best able to help students develop non-cognitive abilities never say a word about the skills in the classroom.

Elizabeth Spiegel, a chess instructor, was profiled in *How Children Succeed* by Paul Tough.[1] The students on her chess team—from an inner-city school—have consistently performed at a very high level, winning national championships over private school students. According to Tough, she conveyed more than chess knowledge to her students; she also communicated a sense of belonging, self-confidence, and purpose. Her students persisted at difficult tasks, overcame great obstacles and dealt with frustration; they persisted on long-term goals even when it seemed impossible to achieve them. Yet, she never addressed Character Strengths directly. She spoke only about chess. She did not even give them pep talks. Instead, she modeled intensity and purpose. She analyzed their game play and talked matter-of-factly about their mistakes. She helped them see what they could do differently. The way she paid careful and close attention to her students' work changed not only their chess ability but also their overall approach to life. Tough concluded Character Strengths are a product of a teen's environment. As we have observed, there is significant evidence that in middle and high school, teens' Character Strengths are a reflection of the home and school environments.

Parents face the same challenge in the context of their relationship with their teen. Parents who want to help their Independence-Building Teen especially need to build their awareness of how the family environment, the school environment, and peer influence may be affecting the teen's behavior.

The Independence-Building Teen will require open communication between parents and school personnel including the school psychologist, school counselor, coaches, teachers, and other important adults to share information about the teen's behavior and performance.

Know where your teen is and what they're doing. Use effective Authoritative Parenting. This includes listening to all of the facts before forming a parental response. Make discipline a corrective experience rather than a form of punishment.

Don't allow the student to manipulate you as a parent by accusing you of not caring enough. This is a blatant attempt to make you feel guilty. Instead, be clear with the student regarding what is right and wrong—what is OK behavior and what is not OK. Don't give sermons on moral issues. Such lectures are counterproductive and serve only to alienate your teen.

Focus on the behavior rather than the attitude. This is a very important distinction. Effective discipline focuses on behavior rather than thoughts or opinions.[2]

Authoritative Parents encourage verbal give and take. They discuss the reasoning behind their policy. They ask the reason if their teen refuses to conform. They express their own perspective as parents but recognize their teen's interests and individual ways.

Authoritative Parents affirm their teen's good qualities and also set high standards for future conduct. They use reason as the basis of discussion about their policies and limits. They do not base decisions on consensus or the teen's desires alone.

The Independence-Building Teen may assert independence by creating a conflict with you. The best approach is to focus on the behavior alone. Do not feed into the conflict or power struggle by demanding respect or obedience even when your teen gives a snarky disrespectful response. Keep the issue of the behavior front and center. Remember that parental authority and guidance is really a service you provide. Pick your "battles." These are not "battles" at all; if you don't fight, there's no one to fight with.

The point of your parental and house rules is to help your student. As Gregory Bodenhamer suggests in his excellent book *Back in Control*, select only a few rules that you feel strongly about and be willing to do what you must to back up these rules with action because these few rules matter most for your teen's well-being.

My Family's Experience

Shelley and I kept these ideas in mind when addressing our kids' behavior. I call it "using the Right Hand and the Left Hand together" when I explain the Authoritative Parenting style to parents in counseling. Using only one hand means you are working with one hand tied behind your back.

The "Right Hand" refers to the "hard power" of rules, discipline, rewards, punishments, and logical consequences in response to a teen's behavior. The "Left Hand" refers to communication, insight, influence, persuasion, Connection Responses, and other "soft power" ways of addressing a teen's behavior. Both are needed, not just one or the other.

Notice Authoritarian Parents use the Right-Hand strategies almost exclusively. Permissive Parents rely on the Left-Hand techniques. The more balanced approach of Authoritative Parents includes both.

Chores and helping out around the house were always an issue in our home. We tried chore charts, rewards, punishments, incentives—nothing seemed to work very well. Then we hit on a simple way to address the issue: We made a short list of the things needing to be done including taking out the trash, sweeping the floor, emptying the dishwasher, etc. We said, "Just pick one chore a day and do it. Pick anything off the list." That's the one that worked the best. The next morning there was a competition to be first to cross off what was considered the easiest chore—taking out the trash. The element that worked here was the Autonomy involved. Each of our kids got to decide which chore to choose. It was "first come, first serve" so anyone could get the chore they wanted if they simply did it first and crossed it off the list. They actually competed to do their favorite chore first!

Missing Assignments

When Shelley and I discussed the missing assignments problem with our teen we saw that forgetfulness was an element. We decided a new arrangement was needed. As you may remember, in this case it was, "Don't come into the car unless you have your book and assignments." This worked because we had direct influence at that moment. The car wouldn't move unless the book and assignments were there! Notice, the action we decided to take follows from the 100 Percent Responsibility Rule. It required action on our part—to remember each day to take the time to check if the book and assignments were there and to know what the assignments were that day. Also, this response fits with the principle of emphasizing learning (in this case the skill of remembering important things) rather than punishment for the sake of punishment. The response addressed the problem itself ("We can't go home unless you remembered the important stuff").

Authority Is a Service

The proper use of authority is a service to those under the authority. This is true on the national level and is especially true in the family environment.

Show the Independence-Building Teen that avoiding school work is hurting them and NOT hurting the teacher or you as a parent. Teens may think they are "winning" if they refuse to work. Acknowledge their need for appropriate independence. Offer areas where they can assert independence and control. Offer appropriate choices.

The Independence-Building Teen and Manipulation

The Independence-Building Teen is one who gets everyone around them to do much of their work, as Tom Sawyer did when he got all the other kids to whitewash the fence for him while he just watched.

Their chief tactic is using vague fuzzy language. They fudge and obscure the rules as much as possible in any given situation. If you try to pin down the Independence-Building Teen to a specific timeline, they will confuse the issue ("Oh, I thought you meant it was due Friday of next week!").

They provide as little information as possible and attempt to make it your fault for the missed assignment. They avoid independence of action at all costs.

The Independence-Building Teen acts as if they have no control over the situation. They hate math and somehow this hatred is not their responsibility. They leave things as vague and non-committal as possible. They passively leave others to clarify the issues. If the issues are left unclear, they readily take advantage it.

The Independence-Building Teen avoids options that would give them freedom and choices in the future since this could lead to independence and responsibility, which are anxiety-provoking for them.

They regularly forget homework, study the incorrect chapter for the test, and lose the directions for an assignment. At the basic level, they fear if they succeed they will be abandoned by their parents. They fear independence and success.

The Independence-Building Teen gets teachers and other authority figures to take on the same function in his life as their parents always have. They consciously or unconsciously manipulate others to take care of them so that they can avoid true independence. They rationalize this as being clever. Others work. They don't. They sit back and are taken care of. College is merely an extended part of adolescence and dependence (that is, if they get into college).

These emotionally-based issues are becoming more and more common in the United States as the world and the economy become more complex. Teens may respond unconsciously—and in many cases consciously—by extending their period of dependence on their family as long as possible.

Some teens come from of a family where there is an approval seeking, hyper-responsible brother or sister to do the household duties the Independence-Building Teen refuses to do or "forgets."

Teachers, coaches and counselors—if they have approval-seeking tendencies—may feel emotionally drained dealing with Independence-Building Teens because they may allow themselves to be manipulated and may become frustrated in attempting to help them.

The Clever Con Artist

As we have observed, the Independence-Building Teen is not lazy and unmotivated; they are highly motivated to achieve the goal of just getting by. They are successfully achieving what they set out to do, which is to just get by so they can avoid more responsibility and avoid facing the future. Since they may not be fully aware of why they are coasting, they easily make excuses for their underperformance. They often fully believe their own excuses!

Scott is a seventeen-year-old who is a truly talented athlete. As an Independence-Building Teen, he received Cs, Ds, and Fs in academic subjects. His football coach became concerned about him. One of his best players—who never had a very good attitude toward authority anyway—was about to become disqualified from playing due to his poor grade point average. Scott told his coach he had been having serious problems at home and had been kicked out of the house on several occasions. He asked his coach if he could have some money to secure a place to stay with friends. His coach gave him one hundred dollars and found out later that the story Scott had told him was untrue.

Scott had frequent run-ins with teachers. His physics teacher was an authoritarian who had served as a sergeant in the US Army before becoming a teacher. Over the course of the semester, this teacher had frequent verbal run-ins with Scott. The teacher had nearly "lost his cool" with Scott a number of times because Scott was frequently defiant and moody in his classroom and made clever, snarky comebacks to the teacher's attempt to confront him in front of the whole class. During one incident, the bell rang for class to be dismissed. There was a very limited time frame during which students had to move from one class to another. Everyone in the classroom knew about the time limit and the fact that students would be in trouble if they were late to their next class. The teacher told everyone they could not leave until he had finished making his caustic comments about those who turned in late assignments in his class. Then he directed his comments toward Scott, escalating to profanity. Scott listened for a few moments. He was seated next to an open window. In an impulsive move, he leaped through the open window, deftly landing a number of feet below outside. He scampered away while the teacher (and Scott's classmates) looked on in amazement. The vice principle was informed and Scott's parents were called in for a conference. His parents were aware of Scott's antics at school and had previously attempted to get him transferred out of the authoritarian teacher's classroom. Fortunately, the vice principal agreed finally to move him into another class when his parents met with her.

Authoritarian teachers are not the only ones who have difficulty with Independence Building students. An approval-seeking teacher may worry about an Independence-Building Teen who accuses her of not spending sufficient time giving instruction, not explaining the material well enough, giving tests that are too difficult, or not giving enough time for assignments.

The Independence-Building Teen and Responsibility

It is important for both parents and teachers not to feel responsible when an Independence-Building Teen doesn't perform. Projecting their responsibility on adults is often the expertise of the teen. If they can make a parent or teacher feel guilty for their actions, the teen can successfully avoid taking any responsibility. As in Scott's case, however, it is also important for parents to discern when it is time for them to intervene with or advocate for their teen.

Some Independence-Building Teens accuse the teachers of ruining their chances of getting into college. They threaten to tell parents and administrators that the teacher is being unreasonable. It is a balancing act that requires careful thought and discernment to determine an Authoritative course of action. Do not rescue an Independence-Building Teen from a teacher exercising appropriate authority over the student. However, advocate for your teen when it is appropriate to do so.

Often the Independence-Building Teen will attempt to make parents feel responsible for everything that happens to them. After all, they did not ask to be born. Parents can respond, "We agree that it was not your choice whether to be born, but since you are here it is up to you to decide what to do with the rest of your life."

Another use of guilt occurs when a teen says they want to find a job. Parents may be happy to hear that they want a job. Yet, if they don't make an honest attempt to find one they may end up finding excuses and placing the responsibility to find a job on the parents. A parent could ask, "How would you go about finding the job you really want?" If they accuse you of not trying to help you can respond, "Finding a job is your responsibility. I am willing to help you."

The Independence-Building student is crafty and clever. They have a deal to offer ("If you get me a new laptop I'll be able to do really well. If you don't, well, I can't work. I'll probably keep getting Fs. That will be your fault").

The Independence-Building Teen often succeeds in escaping responsibility. There is no incentive to figure out why they repeatedly create failure and avoid success. In fact, failure becomes "success" in this topsy-turvy way.

Parents and teachers should not make things easier for the Independence-Building Teen. If teachers decrease the expectations of a course, they only reinforce the belief that external circumstances are the basis for their poor grades.

Authoritative Parenting and the Independence-Building Teen

Authoritative Parents use both "Right Hand" and "Left Hand" approaches with their teen. That is, they set firm limits and, at the same time, maintain good communication with their teen. They encourage verbal give and take and discuss the reasoning behind their rules and policies. They discuss the issues when he refuses to conform. Authoritative Parents enforce limits but also recognize the teen's interests. Authoritative Parents affirm their teen's qualities and set standards for conduct. Although it can be a challenge with an Independence-Building Teen, Authoritative Parents are both warm and firm. They encourage their teen to be independent while maintaining reasonable limits.

Don't invoke the "Because I said so" rule. Instead, listen to your teen's viewpoint and be willing to discuss the reasons behind your rules and policies. Teens learn how to negotiate and engage in discussions when parents take this approach.

Authoritative Parenting is associated with healthy development and provides a balance between affection and support and an appropriate degree of rules and limits in managing behavior. It may seem to you that your teen is simply lazy. However, in reality, they are trying to avoid the pressure of added responsibility. It becomes easier to balance warmth and expectation when you fully realize this "hidden" intent.

Even your teen probably doesn't fully realize why they make excuses and continue underachieving!

In such a situation, the parental responsibility is to create a system for having open communication with the teen's teachers so that all information regarding upcoming assignments and exams is readily available.

Let your teen know that you will be informed of this so you will be able to do regular checks of his or her school work. This includes asking to see the work, not blindly trusting that the work is completed just because your teen says it is.

Some Independence-Building Teens have difficulty solving problems because they actually *think* in vague, fuzzy, and general ways. By encouraging them to clarify, we help them think more clearly about problems in new and more specific ways. They become aware of creative solutions that never occurred to them before if we do not fill in the blanks for them.

Over time, Independence-Building Teens learn the process of clarification and discover solutions for themselves.

Remember that eventually—with patient and proper intervention—the goal is for the Challenge-Averse Teen to own the problem, not you as parents. Offer your teen assistance with assignments, but do not be more invested in the assignment being completed than they are. The Independence-Building Teen needs more structure and expectations, not less.

Progress with the Independence Building Teen

The Independence-Building Teen will deny responsibility in every circumstance ("It's not my fault. The teacher was an idiot. I don't need Algebra to be a plumber").

They deny responsibility for the grade in algebra by saying that the teacher was incompetent. The Independence-Building Teen feels incapable of expressing their anger directly. Instead, they express it through passive-aggressive means, including underperformance, denial, and indifference.

The 100 Percent Responsibility Rule

The 100 Percent Responsibility Rule says, "Take 100 percent of your responsibility in a given situation and take zero percent of the teen's responsibility." What is your responsibility as a parent in this particular situation?

In situations with an Independence-Building Teen, your responsibility as a parent is to avoid the pitfalls and traps the teen places in your way and refuse to take over their responsibility for their work and actions. Moreover, your responsibility as a parent includes using frequent Connection Responses so your teen can reflect upon their own responsibilities.

The Independence-Building Teen may try to manipulate you by saying if you do not help solve their problems the situation will get worse and it will be your fault. It is a balancing act to determine whether to help or allow your teen to face the challenge without your interference.

Be aware that the Independence-Building Teen tends to con and manipulate. They rely on vague general statements that place responsibility on the teacher or you as parents to figure out what they mean. In order to shift the responsibility back to them, it's helpful to ask for clarification when any communication is fuzzy or unclear.

For example, when their teachers ask why they haven't handed in homework, the teen may often say they forgot it. The real reason, of course, is that they evaded the responsibility for handing it in. Instead of challenging the excuses it is better to ask for a clear and more precise explanation of what they mean and wait for a response. Even if no response is forthcoming, the exchange is a way of placing the responsibility where it belongs: with the teen.

Communication: Using Silent Expectation

The simplest way to clarify is to remain silent until the Independence-Building Teen adds to a vague, general statement. Let's say that a student comes into gym class and says to the teacher, "I don't want to do the exercises."

Most coaches would respond, "Get down there right away and do them, or else I'm going to walk you right down to the principal's office." The problem with this response is that it allows the Independence-Building Teen to feel like a victim; the poor student is being bullied by the mean gym coach. Remaining silent and waiting for him to explain what they mean is more effective.

Sometimes "waiting them out" is necessary. The Independence-Building Teen eventually explains and with each succeeding question they will answer more quickly because they know that the coach or teacher expects a complete answer.

Using a Short Response

Another way to handle the Independence-Building Teen who answers vaguely is to give a very short response like "OK . . .?" many times, the less said the better.

Parents and teachers often fall into the trap of lecturing the teen. Independence-Building Teens nearly always have parents who lecture them often, yet do nothing about following through with a well thought out response to the behavior in question.

The Independence-Building Teen learns to ignore authority figures. There is no reason to pay attention since no action will be taken. Instead, be a parent who listens more than speaks. Use a short answer that shows you are listening but places the responsibility on the teen. Ask for clarification.

Remember that these Independence-Building Teens are struggling to identify their own thoughts, much less solve their problems. Asking them to clarify coaxes the teen to sort through their thoughts and consider the problems in new and specific ways. It allows them to discover solutions that wouldn't have occurred to them on their own.

The Connection Response

The Connection Response acknowledges the feeling that underlies their words and encourages your teen to think of other situations in which they felt the same way.

According to research on listening skills, being a good listener means focusing attention on the message and reviewing the important information. Parents can model good listening behavior for their teen and advise them on ways to listen as an active learner, pick out highlights of a conversation, and ask relevant questions. Sometimes it helps to show your teen that an active listener is one who looks the speaker in the eye and is willing to turn the television or smartphone off to make sure the listener is not distracted by outside interference.

Using the Connection Response with the Independence-Building Teen

The Connection Response can be effective in helping the Independence-Building Teen. The Connection Response invites the teen to think about their own feelings and behavior rather than the smokescreen issue they may be using to evade responsibility.

The Independence-Building Teen's poor grades and lackluster performance are often an expression of anger or anxiety.

When an Independence-Building Teen is asked if they completed an assignment, the answer—as we have often seen—is, "Oh, I forgot."

The Connection Response could be, "Hmm, I wonder if you are angry or worried about something . . ." You can leave this message with your teen and they may begin to think about the assertion.

When the teen fails to complete an assignment, you could say, "Hmm, I don't know what you are upset about, but I bet it's something . . ." In this way they are invited to think about the process of avoiding the direct expression of feelings and to look introspectively at their own thoughts and feelings.

Use this approach to avoid the trap of constantly lecturing your teen. Place the responsibility for figuring out what is going wrong squarely on their shoulders. You are implicitly leaving the issue in their hand to solve and you are simultaneously expressing a kind of confidence that they can do it. The game of evading responsibility is short circuited.

The Evading Responsibility Game

The essence of the Independence-Building Teen's "game" of avoiding responsibility has been identified in Transactional Analysis terms as "I'm not OK; you're not OK—Ha! Ha!"[3]

This game is frequently played by rebellious teens, and by alcoholics of all ages in particular. It goes generally like this: The teen does something that is "not OK," such as breaking a school or house rule or not turning in an assignment. The parent or teacher loses their cool and yells at, lectures, or berates the young person.

Any of these courses of action place the adult in the category of "not OK" because none of them are effective. Lecturing the teenager about responsibilities is quite ineffective. The teen walks away feeling "not OK," but he has consolation in the fact that the adult is "not OK" as well. The favorite sport of many Independence-Building Teens is to challenge an adult's authority and walk away after making the adult look like a fool.

The only remedy to the unhealthy game "I'm not OK; you're not OK—Ha! Ha!" is the healthy game "I'm OK; you're OK." Notice the use of the Connection Response is one straightforward way to turn the game the Independence-Building Teen attempts to play into a constructive interaction.

The implicit message given when a Connection Response is used is, "You are going to be OK. I have confidence that you can figure out how you feel, why you feel that way, and how to take responsibility to make some progress." Essentially you are saying, "I have confidence in you."

To be sure, the Right Hand and the Left Hand need to work together. You may offer a small reward for having all assignments done each week, but realize the reward is merely a token to recognize effort. As we know, the reward is not going to be a magic way to change your teen's behavior.

Some parents would say, "Reward? Dr. Mark, you are telling me to bribe my son. He's supposed to do his assignments without a reward!" I explain the difference this way: It's a matter of degree. It's a bribe to say, "Do your homework this week and we will go to Disneyland." It's a proportionate and reasonable reward to say, "Finish your homework first and then I will make dessert." The important work of creating a family environment that encourages intrinsic motivation comes after the reward is or is not earned. Say your teen responds with "I'm gonna eat my candy bar for dessert even if you don't make brownies." You may respond with a Connection Response rather than an attempt to control or up the ante, "You have control over that; it's your candy bar, after all . . ." Notice this is making an educated guess about their state of mind (feeling "in control") but it is not an attempt to coerce.

Crossing the Line

Sometimes the stakes are more serious.

Kyle is thirteen years old. He brought a knife to school and was expelled under the "Zero Tolerance" policy. His parents had to scramble to get him admitted to a charter school that would take him despite the incident on his record. Kyle's action carried its own consequences. He had to start over in a new school. He no longer saw his old friends at school. Since he couldn't drive, he couldn't see his friends outside of school either unless his parents provided transportation. Kyle's parents considered his peers at the old school a "bad influence" so they were not inclined to drive him to meet them on weekends. Kyle was soon focused on meeting new friends at his new school. It was a struggle at first for Kyle and his parents because the charter school meant they had to drive further each day to get him to school. His parents saw there was no reason to add consequences or punishment onto the situation. Kyle fully understood that his actions had resulted in his expulsion and he was very unhappy with the result. He said, "It's unfair!" His parents did not agree or disagree. When he complained about the situation, they used Connection Responses like "You're angry about the situation. We don't like it either."

If the Independence-Building Teen cheats, it is important for his parents NOT to rescue him from the consequences of his actions.

Jackson is an eighteen-year-old senior in high school. He told his parents he wanted to go into the US Army right out of high school. His parents argued with him ("Why don't you go to college and see if you like it? Then you can go into the Army as an officer after you graduate college"). Jackson would hear none of it. He contacted the local recruiter and began to meet with an Army mentor who gave him assignments at the recruitment office.

Jackson soon became so involved at the recruitment office that his grades began to slip. Even though Jackson knew he had to graduate high school to be accepted into the Army, he allowed his math grade to fall into the failing range. At this point his parents were not sure exactly what went on. Since he was eighteen years old, the school would not communicate with his parents without Jackson's written permission. Jackson's dad was incensed ("How can we help him if they won't tell us what's going on? He's screwing up again"). He was angry with Jackson and wanted to consider just asking him to move out. After all, he was already eighteen years old. Jackson's mom was upset with him for even suggesting it.

Next, they found out Jackson had been called into a meeting at the school. He had cheated on his online math class trying to pull out a passing grade at the last moment. Evidently, he bought a code from a peer to get the answers to the final examination. Jackson was given the choice of being expelled from the school or giving up the name of the peer from whom he had bought the code. The peer had sold the code to a number of students and the school administration considered this male peer's offense to be greater than Jackson's. If he gave the principal the male peer's name, Jackson would be allowed to retake the class during the summer. In no case would he be allowed to graduate on time. Jackson agonized over the decision. He said, "I'm no rat!" His dad realized Jackson had faced several consequences of his actions and decided not to intervene other than to listen to Jackson's complaints about the school and his rumination about how stupid the situation was and how he couldn't become a "rat." Jackson didn't volunteer the information to parents, but his recruiter informed Jackson that he would have to create a new recruitment contract. He would have to wait until he graduated high school. He would also be required to fulfill additional conditions before he would be accepted into basic training. This situation was the most significant consequence to Jackson. He had his heart set on the Army. He finally made the decision to "turn state's evidence" (as he put it) on the peer who had been selling the computer code even though he did not want to do it. He enrolled in the course for the summer, got his diploma, and fulfilled his recruitment contract. Notice Jackson's parents did not add any additional consequences or punishments to the natural consequences he faced. They realized accountability was built in. They supported him in the sense that they listened to his thoughts and feelings about the situation he had gotten himself into. They encouraged him to make the right decision. Relatedness, Autonomy, and Competence (the three elements, as you recall, necessary for Character Strengths to develop) were communicated to Jackson. His parents had basic confidence he would be able to move forward in the situation that he found very stressful.

Common Situations with the Independence-Building Teen

Parents and teachers both have an important role to play. However, the most effective way to play that role is to avoid overwhelming the teen with your own anxiety as parents about the underperformance and allow the student to think about and feel their own responsibility in the matter.

A typical way in which Independence Building students may attempt to manipulate parents and teachers is by using deadlines against them.

If an Independence Building student is given an assignment to write two term papers, they will put it off until it's too late and then ask, "Was that assignment for this semester? Gee, I didn't understand. How about I do just one of the papers and you give me credit for both."

The Independence-Building Teen tends to procrastinate. The best way to deal with the procrastination is to require an assignment every day. In this way, the issue comes up frequently and may be dealt with. The Independence-Building Teen will hate these requirements, but they will start learning to how to organize time around the time limits set by teachers and parents.

Procrastination

Sheila is a sixteen-year-old in an advanced English class. The class required a term paper but Sheila's mother knew she did not have the organizational skills to plan her time effectively, do the research, and successfully complete the project. Under the idea of 100 percent responsibility, Sheila's mother thought through the situation ("My responsibility as a parent, knowing what I know about Sheila, is to set up some structure that makes sense. I can't take Sheila's responsibility for completing the work, but I can set up short-term expectations consistent with the 'homework time' she has already agreed to keep daily, and I can check once a day on whether she is doing the work to keep up in the class or not").

She contacted the teacher by email and found that the research for the term paper was organized into small steps, including the process of completing note cards with references to be used in the completed term paper. The syllabus for the course even provided suggested timelines. The steps required to do the research for the term paper, complete note cards, and create an outline were not considered assignments or homework, however. No grades were given for the interim steps. Because it was an advanced class, the teacher considered giving grades for these steps to be "micromanagement" and she refused to do it. Sheila's mother emailed the teacher and asked if she would help to structure Sheila's semester by at least checking her progress regularly. The teacher agreed to do so but repeated her belief that micromanaging a student is not helpful. Without disagreeing, Sheila's mother coordinated with the teacher. She knew when note cards were expected to be complete and when a final outline was expected. She did not offer any specific reward to Sheila if she completed her work each day and each week. But she knew how much work was supposed to be done at week 1, week 2, etc. She was careful to use open-ended Connection Responses and to avoid criticism, "you should" statements, or any other type of communication that could be considered controlling, coercive, or even overly anxious. This was a challenge for Sheila's mom because she was, in fact, quite anxious watching Sheila procrastinate during the first part of the semester. She would merely observe ("I notice you haven't done the three note cards during your homework time. Maybe you don't feel inspired to write about your topic today"). Sheila would often make an excuse ("I have too many other assignments . . ."). Sheila's mom would use the opportunity to make a neutral comment like, "Sometimes it's hard to get yourself to spend the extra moments to finish the day's work" and leave it at that.

Underlying Anxiety

The Independence-Building Teen's core problem is the fear of true independence. Under the surface, they are afraid that their parents will abandon them when they succeed.

The Independence-Building Teen does not generally show outward signs of anxiety, but it is there. They may say they want to succeed but complain they have no control over the matter. As they gain confidence they will start to establish more positive relationships with others. The fear of abandonment will slowly disappear.

When they start to make choices that lead to success they are taking a step into independence of action. Eventually they establish positive mature relationships with peers and stop their attempts to manipulate adults.

Another common situation that the Independence-Building Teen creates involves manipulating other students to do work for him. They may become adept at distracting teachers and parents from the basic issue of the responsibility to complete the academic work. Focus on the responsibility to complete the work, not the manipulation of peers.

If an Independence-Building Teen forgets a notebook and asks the teacher to borrow one, the teacher can simply ignore the request rather than be manipulated into taking care of the student. The behavior may escalate to asking other students for notebook paper or getting other students to allow them to copy their homework assignments.

When the Independence-Building Teen cons other students, they are playing the "I'm not OK; you're not OK—Ha! Ha!" game with the teacher. They are saying, "I'm disrupting your classroom and I wonder whether you can figure out why I am doing this."

If the teacher simply uses disciplinary measures alone by giving the student detention, the game has worked. The teen successfully obscured the issue of personal responsibility to complete the school work. If the teacher attempts to control all misbehavior in the classroom they will fail to impact the Independence-Building Teen. The focus on the issue at hand—misbehavior—is not the cause of the misbehavior.

What can a teacher say in response to such a common situation? It is important for the teacher to focus on the task avoidance. Using a Connection Response can be effective in refocusing the student on the real underlying issue.

The teacher could say, "Interesting how every time you start thinking you can't do something in my class on your own that you try to get another person to take care of you. I wonder why." This comment focuses the attention on the real problem and away from the distraction.

Notice how this uses the "soft power" of influence and insight rather than the "hard power" of force, disciplinary measures, and punishment. It's the Right Hand and the Left Hand working together.

It may take several interactions of this type. If the teacher is persistent, patient, and nonjudgmental, the student may eventually disclose some of the real issues and feelings behind the behavior.

Connection Responses can draw the real issues out into the open. You can point out, "It seems that each time something is really bothering you, you have trouble getting the assignment in on time. I wonder what that means." This places the responsibility on the student to look to their own thoughts and feelings as the source of the behavior.

Key Action Steps ✓

- Focus on the *behavior* rather than the attitude. Use the 100 Percent Responsibility Rule to clarify what you as a parent must do (and NOT do) to allow your teen to learn from each reasonable challenge. Set only rules you can fully back up (not many!) and allow your teen to face natural consequences of their own actions (i.e., face failure).

- Often times, the student will try to assert their independence by creating a confrontation with you. Focusing on the behavior avoids the confrontation and keeps the issue of the behavior front and center.

- Show your teen that avoiding school work is actually harmful to him or her, not to the teacher or to you as a parent. Explain—when the subject arises—that it's not "winning" if they refuse to work or do their assignments.

- Acknowledge your teen's need for appropriate independence and offer areas where he or she can exert his or her independence and control.
- Use Connection Responses to focus on your teen's strengths that are not being taken advantage of. For example, you might say "Tom, you are really good at getting to your basketball practice on time and you have been really committed to the team, but I've noticed this doesn't happen with your math homework." After making such a statement, follow up with more Connection Responses to home in on your teen's feelings and thoughts.
- Do not make suggestions or criticisms. Avoid confrontations.
- Know the personality of the Challenge-Averse Teen. They are not lazy and unmotivated; they are highly motivated to achieve the goal of just getting by. They are successfully achieving what they set out to do. They avoid responsibility and avoid facing the future.
- Remember that this teen has outsmarted him or herself. They may not be fully aware of why they are coasting and avoiding responsibility. They may fully believe their own rhetoric and excuses.
- Make a system for having open communication with the teen's instructors so that all information regarding upcoming assignments and exams is readily available.
- Let your teen know you will be informed, so you will be able to do regular checks of his or her school work. This includes asking to see the work, not blindly trusting that the work is completed just because they say it is.
- Remember that the teen—rather than the parent—needs to own the problem. They may receive assistance with assignments, but the parent should not be more invested in the assignment being completed than the student is.
- Ask your teen the following open-ended question, "Are you getting the grades you want this semester?" This helps the student discuss his or her goals.

- When having a conversation be sure that the motivation is to help him or her, not to belittle or challenge in a way that will result in an argument. This includes focusing on the facts and encouraging them to participate in solving the problem.

CHAPTER 6

The Initiative-Building Teen

Anthony is a seventeen-year-old who loves to skateboard and binge-watch television shows. He occasionally smokes pot, but doesn't consider it a problem. He has fallen behind in high school credits, and has been asked by the school administration to make up the credits online so he would be in range to graduate just one year late if he attended summer classes. Even though he is in danger of not graduating high school, he appears unconcerned. He projects a "mellow" personality. He seldom initiates conversation with adults but is quite popular with peers. As far as he was concerned, there really was no problem with his school situation. Sure, he was a little behind in school. Who wasn't? "No need to get all upset," he'd say.

His parents were much more concerned about his academic underperformance than he appeared to be. They had spent time and money attempting to arrange a summer class at an expensive non-public school so he could make up his deficient credits. Anthony, for his part, went along with attending the summer class, but didn't finish the assignments. His parents' efforts were wasted. Anthony just shrugged. He said he had done his best and it wasn't a big deal.

The Initiative-Building Teen is one of the most common types of Challenge-Averse Teens. They do just enough to get by. Often, it's extremely frustrating for a parent to watch. By the end of the semester, the Initiative-Building Teen can sometimes pull out a passing grade, sometimes not.

The Initiative-Building Teen usually starts the school year OK, since long-term assignments are not due. They don't do homework, so math classes are often the first indicator of a problem. They are not especially defiant or negative about missing assignments. The Initiative-Building Teen shows these behaviors at the beginning of middle school when longer term projects are routinely assigned. They are expert procrastinators. They have a million plausible reasons for poor grades and late assignments. They seem to believe that if they don't try hard and fail, it's not really failure. After all, they never really tried! In this way, they protect their self-esteem.

Building Motivation

Anthony's parents tried everything to motivate him. The trouble was their understanding of the relationship between motivation and performance was, in fact, backwards.

It seems quite common sense to ask, "When Anthony gets motivated, he'll do his school work; but how do we motivate him?" This question contains a basic error in thinking that many people make when thinking about motivation. It seems only logical that motivation must come first in order to perform. The problem is this overcomplicates the process. It requires two steps—first motivation, and then performance. The error in thinking is that, somehow, we must first know how to motivate the teen. Then, they will engage in some manner of psychological effort that results in getting up and doing the assignments.

Here is how to actually "motivate" an Initiative-Building Teen to do their assignments. Get the assignment started in a reliable way— even if this means sitting down with your teen to assist them in getting started. We know this by itself is not a long-term solution. As soon as you leave, they will often stop doing the assignment.

However, in the process of doing the assignment, they will often discover some value in doing the task. Your teen will naturally feel good about at least getting part of it done. It's a relief to a teen with a procrastination habit, for example, to get a project off to a start.

The real motivation comes from this feeling of accomplishment and relief. They must fully experience and note the internal motivation that comes from the *action* of doing the task at hand. The doing comes first. The motivation follows. The real issue is creating an overall environment in which your teen begins to feel this motivation, takes note of it, and begins to act on it.

Understand, though, that there's a process involved in discovering internal motivation. Initiative-Building Teens may get a number of tasks started even on their own, but they do not follow through. The reason for dropping the assignment is that they do not notice their own positive feelings and motivation when they get something done ("It's never enough [for my parents, my teachers]"). They may think, "It's so little compared to all I have to get done." They may have innumerable other thoughts that tend to squelch motivation as well.

It would be so nice if we, as parents, could simply re-program a teen's mind like a computer. Hit the delete button on these negative kinds of thoughts and insert the positive and motivation-building kind of thoughts. For example, the remedies for the two statements above are as follows: "It doesn't have to be 'enough' for anyone else. *If I* am satisfied with the amount of work I got done, I can declare this session a success! *I* get to decide that" and, "It's not necessarily 'so little.' Just get a bit done each day and it amounts to quite a lot over a number of days." Parents often say these kinds of things. Why doesn't it just work?

There is a process known as cognitive restructuring (fancy words for "thought change"), in which the therapist helps, say, a person with anxiety symptoms to change their thoughts from negative anxiety-producing thoughts to more positive, rational thoughts.

Cognitive therapy has become very popular with good reason. Research shows cognitive behavioral therapy (CBT) works as well as psychoactive medication in clinical trials. Moreover, certain types of so-called dysfunctional thoughts are shown to lead to particular problems. In general, "loss thoughts" lead to depression, "unfair thoughts" lead to anger, and negative predictions about the future lead to anxiety.

If only direct, CBT could just change a teen's pattern of thought! Certainly, many parents give positive and motivating messages to their teens quite often. So why doesn't it work?

Remember Elizabeth Spiegel from the last chapter? As a chess instructor, she created an environment for the disadvantaged students on her chess team which somehow helped them to perform at a very high level. She communicated a sense of relatedness, self-confidence, and purpose. Her students persisted at difficult tasks, overcame great obstacles, and dealt with frustration. They persisted on long-term goals, even when it seemed impossible to overcome the odds.

Most interestingly, she never gave pep talks. She didn't address their thoughts and beliefs. She did not attempt to change the negative dysfunctional beliefs her students may have been thinking. Yet, the evidence is clear. Her students ended up changing their thought patterns *themselves*. How did this occur?

How Change Happens

Ms. Spiegel provided the environment which encouraged and enabled the students to make the changes within themselves. It became "an inside job." Only the teen themselves can do this inside job. As parents, we can't do it directly. We can only provide the proper environment. Fortunately, research and experience say this is enough.

The important idea here is this: teens don't get motivated and then do something. Rather, they do something and then get motivated. Motivation doesn't precede performance. It is just the opposite: *Performance must come first.* It precedes the motivation, and the process becomes a positive cycle. It is in the process of performing the action that teens discover their motivation.

Paradoxically, it is not important or even really possible to motivate your Initiative-Building Teen with some kind of magic words or a set of clever manipulations. Your concern as a parent is merely to get the desired behavior started, not change the mindset of your Initiative-Building Teen. And an additional bonus comes quite naturally. When behavior changes, thoughts change.

Steve and His Parents

Steve was a fourteen-year-old ninth-grader who was not doing his homework. Consequently, he was failing most of his classes. Sure, he'd pull out a D or even a C in some of his classes by the end of the semester, but he was clearly not working up to his potential. His parents were angry with him. His mom feared for his future. After all, he was in the first year of high school and the GPA would count toward college admission.

His father argued with Steve almost every night after he had asked him whether he had done his assignments. He punished Steve, grounding him for the entire semester. They even engaged in a screaming match, which was very disturbing to Steve's mom. None of his parents' interventions worked.

During a session with Steve, I discovered he liked board games. I offered him the following assignment: At the end of each school day, he was to play a game called "Spin the Wheel" on one of his favorite board games. He was to write down all of his classes and assign a number for each. He would then spin the wheel and do the homework only for the one class the wheel indicated. He seemed interested and agreed to do it.

His parents were rather upset by the assignment. They asked me how this would get him to do all of his homework. I explained that my interest was in getting something started. I outlined the research on motivation, Character Strengths, and the family environment. When they returned for their counseling session in two weeks, Steve had completed one assignment each night as he had agreed to do.

I asked if he might be interested in adding one additional assignment. Steve said, "I'm good" with completing just one.

His parents were quite upset with me. If Steve completed only one assignment per night, this would guarantee continued failure! When they returned two weeks later, Steve had still been doing only one assignment per night. However, by the following session—just a month after the initial challenge—he was doing all of his homework. This appeared to be some kind of miracle.

I made an open-ended Connection Response in this latest session with Steve, observing that he had decided to do more of his assignments and wondering how he felt about it. For his part, Steve was more forthcoming than I had ever seen him. He said, "Actually, when I turned in my homework, a girl in my math class talked to me out of the blue. She said, 'I kind of thought you were a dillweed[1] until I saw you taking your homework so seriously.'"

From then on, he got his homework done. He caught fire! Since Steve was a very perceptive young guy, he saw that his peers, both male and female, had begun to see him differently. Things were undeniably better at home. He also began to feel more motivated to finish his assignments.

Notice Steve began to feel and note his *own* motivation. No one could talk him into doing his homework. The change was not the result of punishment, reward, or pep talks. He was not coerced or incentivized into making the change.

The Family Environment and the Initiative-Building Teen

Research has shown that motivation is a function of the family (and school) environment. Essentially, the *relationships* of the teen create the human environment in which they function.

Deci and Ryan, the Self-Determination Theory (SDT) researchers, performed experiments to show the validity of their ideas. They found, in the long run, it is important for students to *internalize* their motivation. Specifically, they found when parents and teachers are able to create an environment that promotes feelings of Autonomy, Competence, and Relatedness, teens show much higher levels of intrinsic motivation.

Teens experience Autonomy when their parents emphasize a sense of choice, while minimizing feelings of coercion and control. Steve's mom and (particularly) dad were able to let go of their attempts to coerce, cajole, and control him. They largely stopped arguing with him about homework. They didn't attempt to convince him of the importance of good grades. They went along with the exercise I gave him—to make a free will choice about whether to do one assignment or none—even though they didn't like it at first.

Teens feel Competent when their parents give them tasks that they can succeed at, but that are not too easy—reasonable challenges just beyond their current abilities. As a result of letting go of their parental expectations and allowing Steve to decide to do just *one* of his assignments per day, Steve was able to feel competent and successful at finishing one task a day. It was a start, and it gave Steve the emotional space needed to feel his natural motivation after he had accomplished something.

Finally, teens feel a sense of Relatedness when they perceive that their parents like, value, and respect them. Steve's parents had become so angry and frustrated with him that he no longer sensed his parents' affection. Quite the opposite had taken hold in the family home. Each day was tense and unpleasant. Steve didn't believe his dad liked him anymore. He did not feel Relatedness in his home.

When Steve's parents followed the plan I had outlined, the arguments and yelling stopped. For his part, Steve's dad had begun to plan in some positive individual time with him as I had suggested. They threw the football in the backyard. They even went fishing as they had done when Steve was much younger.

Those three feelings, as Deci and Ryan have uncovered in their research, are more effective motivators for teens than any external or material rewards.

My Family's Experience

When Alex went to a non-public school for the first time, I was quite concerned that the academic work would be "dumbed-down" and he would fall even further behind than he already was. The schoolwork he brought home only confirmed my fears. It was several grade levels lower than his public-school grade level! I couldn't help thinking I had made the wrong move in getting him into that school.

As it turned out, though, it was necessary for the teachers and other professionals working with Alex to find his baseline in several academic areas (as I actually knew!) but being that Alex was *my* son I still found it quite stressful to watch.

As a result of discovering his personal academic baseline, Alex found a sense of competence in the school since he could do the academic work and the assignments. The work was no longer so far above his ability level that he felt discouraged. When the proper instructional level was found for each subject area, the work was not too easy either. It was in the Goldilocks Zone: just right to challenge him, but not too difficult to accomplish.

"Motivating" an Initiative-Building Teen

We have seen it is not possible or advisable to attempt to "motivate" a Challenge-Averse Teen. Instead, the goal is to develop the type of relationship between the two of you that sets up the three critical elements of Relatedness, Autonomy, and Competence. This requires a close examination of your relationship with your teen to determine if your relationship is indeed cultivating feelings of Relatedness, Autonomy, and Competence.

This kind of relationship with your teen is not one in which you, as an authority, treat the behavior of your teen as a subordinate. Rather, it is a relationship in which you begin to develop the kind of positive relationship you will have with your teen in the near future as they become an adult. Your teen is in the natural process of moving away from you. They are becoming an independent adult, becoming their own person.

It is also quite natural to feel some anxiety as the process unfolds. That's why so many parents tell me they would like their teen to magically disappear for a few days and reappear as an adult. If only it were that easy! There is a natural fear of feeling that your teen is slipping away from you. You no longer have firm control as a parent. Your teen must take over the control for their own life.

Thankfully, there is also a sense of well-being here as a parent. Your job is nearing completion. It's a truly great feeling when your teen is nearing independent adult life.

A Part of Your Relationship

The way people talk about motivation suggests it is exclusively a personal trait of an individual ("He's unmotivated" or "She's a real go-getter!"). It implies the belief that motivation is inside the individual. Research on motivation suggests that this is simply not the case. Lecturing, pep talks, and trying to "get in the head" of your teen won't work. There are sometimes exceptions to this rule, but they are rare.

Motivation is really a product of the family environment—a part of your relationship with your teen. Sure, the eventual goal is internal motivation. Motivated people go outside themselves to seek motivating situations. If they feel uninspired, they go out and find inspirational situations. But when young people are first learning this non-cognitive skill, they learn it from their environment. That's from you and me, as parents—and, hopefully, from teachers also. As we have discussed, they can only effectively learn it in an environment that fosters Relatedness, Autonomy, and Competence.

Deadlines and the Initiative-Building Teen

Let's talk about the best way to approach deadlines with the Initiative-Building Teen. Specific assignments with a timeline can provide an opportunity to have a positive influence, but this requires parents to be in contact with the teen's teachers to coordinate efforts. These situations include an impending major test (such as a midterm or final), an upcoming major assignment due date, project due date, report cards, and a parent conference with the teacher. In these situations, a deadline has appeared.[2]

Since Initiative-Building Teens avoid responsibility, it is important for you to obtain the class syllabus, major assignment deadlines, class requirements, and a summary of the grading system from each teacher. It is common to be able to get this information from the school or the teacher's website. But if it's not, do not hesitate to contact each teacher by email to set up an accountability system. Set up a structure with the teacher and your teen, and be consistent with it.

For example, the most user-friendly system I have found is the daily homework time; just one hour a day that focuses the issue of academics down to the one time when it is the topic to discuss. As we have observed, it is best to drop the topic for the rest of the day, so the issue doesn't continue to negatively affect your relationship with your teen.

Of course, your approach during this hour matters as well. Talk to your son or daughter in a matter-of-fact way ("I know you have this assignment coming due"). Don't accept excuses. Rather, hold your teen accountable. Your approach will demonstrate your patience and consistency. The ultimate goal is for your teen to take full responsibility and ownership for their actions.

The Connection Response

Remember, the Connection Response helps teens to acknowledge the feelings that underlie their words and encourages them to think of other situations in which they may have felt the same. In other words, the Connection Response helps kids feel *emotionally connected*—both to their parents and to their own feelings.

As we have observed, being a good listener means focusing attention on your teen. Of course, it means putting down your cell phone and shutting down the laptop. It also means refraining from formulating an answer while your teen is talking. Rather, your focus, attention, and thoughts are centered on your teen.

As parents, we can listen, pick out highlights of a conversation, and make a good Connection Response as a way of modeling good listening behavior for kids.

I have observed good communication is the primary way parents create an environment that encourages Relatedness, Autonomy, and Competence.

Samuel and His Dad

Samuel, a fourteen-year-old, told me, "My dad just doesn't listen to me." For his part, Samuel's dad, Joseph, told me he didn't think Sam listened to *him*. He wondered why he had to repeat himself over and over, especially when it came to reminding him about chores and homework.

I discussed Connection Responses with him and gave him several examples. Although he was a highly intelligent man, I had to do quite a lot of role play in sessions with Joseph since he had not mastered the art of formulating and using Connection Responses. It turned out his own dad did not really listen to him when he was a teen.

"My dad never looked at me twice," Joseph said. I thought that was incredibly sad, and I told Joseph my feelings about it. He just shrugged and said, "That's the way my dad was." Joseph learned quickly to focus on "feeling words" in what Samuel said to him. I explained that feeling words are generally pretty simple (mad, sad, glad, etc.) and, in contrast, thoughts could be quite complex. "Keep it simple" was my mantra with Joseph. Don't overwhelm Samuel with your thoughts about his thoughts. Just a simple acknowledgment of his feelings would be just great for a start.

I also gave Joseph my usual assignment for parents: Avoid too many questions. Make only Connection Responses to start with. We worked on the kind of things he might say to Samuel.

Joseph reported he didn't get much from Samuel when he tried talking with him this way. He lapsed back into questioning Samuel to get him to say more about his day at school, but this just seemed to cause him to stop talking entirely. It was a long and slow process for Joseph to learn that it would be much more helpful in the long run to stick with non-intrusive Connection Responses rather than questions.

After weeks of one-word answers from Samuel, Joseph finally reported to me that he was starting to open up. He volunteered a little more information about what happened at school. Progress was very slow. I observed that Samuel was, by temperament, a very quiet and self-contained person. Joseph agreed that a forcible attempt to "pry open" the door to Samuel's heart was exactly the wrong approach. But, he needed a lot of support and encouragement to be patient with him.

The 100 Percent Responsibility Rule

The 100 Percent Responsibility Rule says, "Take all of your responsibility in a given situation and take none of the teen's responsibility." I always ask myself, "What is my responsibility, as a parent, in this particular situation?"

With an Initiative-Building Teen, your responsibility is to use frequent Connection Responses so that your teen can reflect upon their own responsibility. The Initiative-Building Teen will avoid talking about the issues or may try to manipulate by "coasting" around the issue.

Be aware that the Initiative-Building Teen (like the Independence-Building Teen) tends to con and manipulate. Vague, general statements can be clarified with a response like, "So, your responsibility in this case is to do what, exactly?" Once your teen has committed (at least verbally) to take action, help them to set a real timeline to actually do it. And be willing to do your part.

This doesn't mean doing it for them. In general, it means you commit to do something that is helpful and supportive. For example, it may mean saying something like, "I will give you one reminder, and then I will ask you once, later, to see if you got it done."

Communication: Using Time Delay

Often, one of the best ways to respond is not to say anything at all, but rather to wait a short time. Let's say your teen has committed to take the trash out to the curb each week. It's the night before trash day and it's getting late. You say, "I notice you haven't taken out the trash bin yet." It is often much better to leave the immediate area rather than watch like a hawk to see if there is a response immediately to your observation. Instead, go about your business and do something else, but after half an hour or so, check to see if the bin was taken out.

If not, you can decide whether to issue another reminder or not, and if so, how to do it. I like to inject some humor into the situation. I may ask, in a mock British "butler" accent, "Suh, may I take out the trash, suh?" My son, Dylan, will respond in a mock accent, "Yes, Jarvis, take it out this instant!" I won't take out the trash for him, but I have—without appearing coercive—made the point that I noticed he did not do what he said he would do.

Using Short, Connecting Responses

Another way to handle the Initiative-Building Teen who answers vaguely is to give a very short response. This invites your teen to clarify their vague statements. Since the Initiative-Building Teen learns to ignore authority figures, it is much better to say little or nothing, rather than lecture or make idle threats to take action. Instead, listen carefully and think about what positive action to take in response to any given situation.

Some Initiative-Building Teens (like Independence-Building Teens) have difficulty because they *actually think* in vague and general ways! Let them come up with specific solutions or proposals, and use a Connection Response to feed back to them what may be helpful.

When Samuel said, "I really need some extra money," at first his dad, Joseph, wanted to say, "Sounds like you need a job" in response. Instead, he thought over what he and I had talked about, and he decided to go with a Connection Response instead, basically feeding back to Samuel his feelings ("Sounds like there's something you want to buy"). In this way, Joseph gave Samuel the space to make the connection that a job may be the solution.

The short Connection Response acknowledges the feeling that underlies your teen's words and encourages the Initiative-Building Teen to think of other situations in which he has *felt* the same way.

As we have observed, parents can model good listening behavior for their teen and advise them on ways to listen as an active learner, pick out highlights of a conversation, and ask relevant questions. Connection Responses are effective in helping the Initiative-Building Teen to think about their own feelings and behavior.

An Initiative-Building Teen is apt to say, "Oh, I forgot" quite often as an excuse. Rather than becoming angry or annoyed, a Connection Response could be, "Looks like you are distracted. Could be you are thinking about something a lot." You open the way for your teen to self-disclose what may be bothering them in this way.

Of course, using this approach avoids the trap of lecturing or being constantly annoyed with your teen. It also places the responsibility for figuring out what is going on with them.

The Initiative-Building Teen's Evading-Responsibility Game

As we saw with the Initiative-Building Teen, the "game" of avoiding responsibility has been identified as "I'm not OK; you're not OK!– Ha! Ha!" But it's different for the cool-headed Initiative-Building Teen. The Independence Builder may do something that is "not OK," like breaking a school or house rule or not turning in an assignment, and wait for his parent to lose their cool. In contrast, the Initiative Builder coasts around issues and seldom chooses confrontation.

Samuel, being an Initiative Builder, would simply grunt in response to Joseph's attempt to make a statement about his assignments. Joseph would remind Samuel when the homework time they had agreed upon started, which for them was six p.m., after dinner ("I bet it's easier to keep up with your homework now that we have this regular quiet homework time set aside").

When Joseph later discovered that Samuel had actually done none of his assignments for three days running and had hidden the fact, he wanted to go ballistic. Instead, he remembered the whole point of setting up the time and using his new communication skills to provide an environment with Relatedness, Autonomy, and Competence. He simply observed, "So, looks like you have had some trouble doing what you said you would do. I wonder what has distracted you so much." Samuel grunted again and avoided answering. But Joseph was glad he did not fall into his old way of responding with anger and recriminations.

In this situation, Samuel's "not OK" behavior of not doing his homework was glaringly obvious after it was discovered. Samuel did not put it "in the face" of his dad, but tried to hide it. Joseph, for his part, could tell there was something different about their interaction this time. Samuel non-verbally acknowledged that he did not live up to his side of the agreement to do his homework. Instead of a cool or snarky remark, Samuel had little to say. Joseph realized lecturing Samuel would have been quite counterproductive.

In the past, Samuel would have felt "not OK" after the tongue-lashing but would not admit it. And Samuel would secretly enjoy pulling the wool over his dad's eyes once again while getting him to go off on him—making Joseph "not OK" as well.

Joseph recognized that the healthy game ("I'm OK; you're OK") was the best way to handle it. It was a serious discussion, even though it took less than a minute. In effect, Joseph had said, "I notice you simply didn't do the homework as you said you would." His response laid the responsibility for figuring out why at the feet of Samuel. He was not letting Samuel off the hook. Quite the opposite; he had noticed his son's behavior and had expressed concern as to why he behaved in this way. Joseph had cleared the air. The message Joseph had given Samuel is, "You are going to be OK. I have confidence that you can figure out how you feel, why you feel that way, and how to take responsibility to make some progress."

During the next session, Joseph asked me whether he should go back and change the rule about homework time, since it wasn't working. After all, Samuel ignored his homework for three days and nothing happened as a consequence. Joseph had already offered a small reward for Samuel keeping his homework current.

We discussed the fact that an additional reward or punishment would probably have no effect. So, Joseph decided to continue with the status quo. The very next session, Joseph reported that Samuel had begun to make some changes on his own. He was still quite uncommunicative, but he had kept up on his daily assignments, which represented great progress for him.

Key Action Steps ✓

- Encourage your teen to make goals that represent small, reasonable challenges.
- Strike a balance between assisting the student and encouraging independence. Figure it out using the 100 Percent Responsibility Rule. It is important not to allow the Initiative-Building Teen to "coast" under the radar. Matter-of-factly note progress or lack of progress and follow with a Connection Response.
- The Initiative-Building Teen needs to be approached in gentle manner. Listen, use Connection Responses, be supportive, and avoid direct criticism.
- Help them to learn to have realistic expectations and time lines, so they stay focused on the completion of their projects. This may be accomplished by helping the teen make an outline for the task or assignment, which includes what he or she is trying to accomplish at each stage.
- They need to be approached in a supportive manner, which does not further contribute to their hidden anxieties about performance. Use supportive, encouraging language.
- Find out the issue(s) behind procrastination behavior, or at least help them figure it out for themselves.
- When approaching the teen's procrastination, it is best to focus on listening to his or her feelings rather than comment on how to do better.
- Encourage your teen to exercise and increase physical activity.
- Supportively and *gently* counter negative beliefs. Don't try to "fix" their negative thinking; instead, be encouraging and supportive of their feelings. Use Connection Responses.
- Don't give false praise. In fact, avoid giving criticism of any type. The Initiative-Building Teen will interpret this in a negative manner.

CHAPTER 7

The Identity-Building Teen

D iana is a very intelligent sixteen-year-old. Her father had achieved a high level of success as a real estate developer. Her mother was a corporate attorney. Diana's older sister had been accepted to an Ivy League college. But even though Diana was identified by her school district as gifted in the fifth grade, she had never achieved a high level of academic success. When I spoke with Diana, she claimed she never liked school. She said she would rather spend her time talking with friends and working on art projects.

Her parents said her grades were relatively good in elementary school, but she began to have difficulty when she entered the sixth grade. Her grades plummeted from As and Bs to Cs and Ds when she entered middle school. Her parents thought it was the adjustment to the new school at first, but her performance remained uneven for years after her transition to middle school. Halfway through the eighth-grade year, Diana was removed from advanced classes as a result of her poor grades. Her academic difficulty continued through her first years of high school, and in the ninth grade she received her first F in algebra. She didn't seem to mind at all. She claimed many of her friends were failing classes. And while her math grades were plummeting, she focused on her interest in ecology. She received good grades in classes that interested her, such as environmental science.

Diana is an Identity-Building Teen. Although she came from a family of high achievers, she was not interested in applying herself at school. She spent her time intensely exploring issues with older friends who were involved in soliciting funds for Greenpeace. She worked diligently on art projects related to her interest in ecology. She worked hard in environmental science and claimed she would pursue a degree after she had some "life experience."

The Identity-Building Teen is focused on figuring out who they are and what they believe. These young people are typically very aware of social issues. They experiment with different styles of dress and different groups of friends. They may believe that other family members are too successful to compete with—so they drop out of the competition. They explore where they might fit in and belong in the larger society. They generally have no clear plan of action or path, but express their ideas passionately as a way to define their beliefs as quite distinct from their parents'.

The Identity-Building Teen is the only one of the Five Types who will eventually grow out of the academic underperformance behavior without specific intervention. As they come to understand their interests and the corresponding prerequisites, the Identity-Building Teen will develop the motivation and ambition to work hard in academic and other pursuits largely on their own. As such, they are a small minority of the Challenge-Averse Teen population.

The Identity-Building Teen should be approached with respect, openness, and acceptance. Learn how to listen in a non-judgmental, non-confrontational, and empathic manner, which includes using Connection Responses.

Diana and Her Parents

Diana's parents, John and Patricia, were both very intelligent and very successful. They were frankly perplexed with Diana's behavior. If she wanted to set a goal to be an environmental scientist, surely she knew she must get good grades to get into college and earn positions she wanted to go.

Her dad, John, was normally working very long hours as a real estate developer. Patricia told me that Diana's dad was so busy and driven that "being married to him is like owning a race horse!" But she tried to compensate for the fact that John was not around much by spending extra time with Diana. She would engage Diana in conversations about current affairs and politics. She agreed with most of the observations Diana made about the world and the corruption she saw in government and politics. Yet, when it came to motivating herself to do something productive, Diana would usually opt out.

Diana would spend hours with older friends raising funds and handing out pamphlets for Greenpeace. She would do assignments only for subjects that interested her.

Diana's mother couldn't help expressing her opinion openly and honestly with Diana ("If you don't make a solid plan to achieve your goals, you will get nowhere"). At this point in the conversation, the communication would break down. Diana withdrew into a typical set of statements ("You don't understand, Mom." "You can't plan my life for me." "You and Dad can just do what you do; I need to do what I have to do!").

Approaching the Identity-Building Teen

The Identity-Building Teen is involved in a struggle to figure out who they are and where they are going. This type appears in mid- to late-adolescence. In essence, the Identity-Building Teen is experiencing a kind of early "mid-life crisis." They may appear to be lazy, but in fact, they are spending most of their energy searching for their purpose in life. They may appear to be intensely self-absorbed and passionate about social causes. They often have dreams and quite grandiose plans. They may agonize over politics and experiment with extreme opinions and beliefs.

Although the Identity-Building Teen expresses passionate opinions and beliefs, they may rarely resolve anything. When it comes to academics, Identity-Building Teens are highly motivated to succeed in some subjects, but not in others. It depends on the value they give to the subject, whether they enjoy it, and whether they are able to actually do the work. They are in a continuous search to determine what is meaningful and to avoid what they consider meaningless.[1]

For example, if your Identity-Building daughter has decided to become a worker for CARE International, she will work hard in International Women's Studies classes, but will not put much effort into reading American Literature, which has nothing to do with her goal. Her parents' role is to help her realize every subject is relevant to understanding the real world. The problem is, the Identity-Building Teen doesn't really want anyone's advice or help. The most effective way to help is through listening and using Connection Responses.

If a parent questions the Identity-Building Teen consistently, the usual interactions can become quite confrontational. Often, this may result in shutting down communication altogether ("Why didn't you study for the math test?" "Why are you wasting your time on everything else and avoiding the important work?"). Confrontational questions like these just create more resistance without helping the situation. These are unproductive ways to interact with your teen. She will tend to "dig in her heels." It's frustrating to watch when your teen is neglecting important work in favor of what seems frivolous. However, a subtler approach is much more productive.

Instead, ask non-specific, open-ended questions. Ask about her point of view and opinion. Be genuinely interested. This may include questions such as, "What is your opinion on that subject?" or "What are your thoughts on your English grade this semester?"

Researcher and UC Berkley professor Ron Dahl wrote about using a proven technique in clinical psychology known as Motivational Interviewing with teens to address difficult problems like drug and alcohol abuse, eating disorders, and risky sexual behavior.[2] He has also suggested it could be helpful for less severe problems.[3] Dr. Dahl makes specific suggestions from the Motivational Interviewing playbook that happen to line up perfectly with the methods other researchers have identified. Let's look at his list:

1. Make an empathic connection
2. Ask open-ended questions
3. Use reflective listening
4. Use non-confrontational ways to point out inconsistencies
5. Support Autonomy and their sense of choice
6. Join Resistance: that is, don't directly disagree with what is said but instead pick out the part you can agree with as much as you can. Emphasize where you agree.
7. Be genuine and value the teen's viewpoint
8. Shift the intensity of the discussion
9. Re-state their opposing viewpoint, and
10. When they are ready, help make a plan of action.

Sound familiar? These principles line up perfectly with the ideas we have already discussed including Self-Determination Theory, Authoritative Parenting, Connection Responses, and the 100 Percent Responsibility Rule. Let's look at applying them with the Identity-Building Teen.

I'm not suggesting that you, as a parent, must become a clinician using the Motivational Interviewing technique perfectly. Rather, borrow some of the approaches Dr. Dahl suggests.

Your teen may express opinions that don't make sense to you, but use some of the Motivational Interviewing ideas to look beyond the superficial to the feeling level of what she is saying. The use of

Connection Responses will open communication with the Identity-Building Teen by giving the message that her ideas are important.

Many times, a parent's first reaction would be to lecture the Identity-Building Teen on straightening her priorities. Instead a Connection Response will let her know that her ideas are important and will open a valuable channel of communication.

Alexa and Francine

I worked with an idealistic nineteen-year-old young woman named Alexa when her mother became concerned about falling grades in school. She told her mom, Francine, "I can't concentrate on school right now. It just doesn't look so important compared to the bigger issues of poverty and social injustice."

I reviewed some of the Motivational Interviewing concepts with Francine. She decided to try her best to use them with Alexa the next time the subject of her academic work came up and Alexa said something like, "Mom, I just don't see the point of school work when there are so many important issues to think about."

Francine responded, "You're having a really tough time concentrating on school work when you are so concerned about poverty and social injustice."

She used the Connection Response as a sincere reflection of Alexa's opinion and feelings without judgment. Next, Francine asked an open-ended question to encourage Alexa to discuss further why she felt so strongly about these issues (idea 2). Here's the gist of another one of their conversations. Notice how many Motivational Interviewing principles Francine was able to use:

> Francine: What are your thoughts on your grades this semester?
>
> Alexa: I can't concentrate on school right now. Not when people are dying.
>
> Francine: You're having a tough time concentrating on school work when you are concerned about poverty and injustice. That's a lot to take on. How do you want to help?

Alexa: Well, I'm trying to get really involved with the Fistula Foundation that raises money and awareness.

Francine: That sounds like a worthwhile group. What do you need to join the group? Do they want people with any skills or education?

Alexa: I guess they hire college graduates. They really need doctors.

Francine: Do you think you want to go to college then?

Alexa: Maybe. But I really want to help people now.

Francine: How about we work together to find a way to balance both? We can figure out what you need to do to get the degree that would help you get a job at this organization or a similar one, and in the meantime I'd like to help you with your volunteer work.

Francine helped Alexa make a plan of action with some short-term goals to get involved with local volunteer work. She actually became involved herself in raising money for the Fistula Foundation. But she also helped her daughter to see how working on long-term goals, like success in school and getting into a good college program, requires attention and dedication. Alexa learned how to balance her concerns about major problems as well as keep up with school work.

Perhaps equally important, the connection and communication between Alexa and Francine was strengthened, and Alexa didn't feel like she was in competition with her parents. Rather, she felt supported in exploring who she was and what was important to her, because her mom showed genuine interest in Alexa's concerns.

Francine used Connection Responses to build a solid sense of Relatedness with Alexa. She used some of the Motivational Interviewing ideas to give Alexa a sense of Autonomy and Competence. And her genuine interest in helping Alexa with fund-raising was based on her reading of the 100 Percent Responsibility Rule; Francine really re-examined her own beliefs and actions in response to her daughter's ideals. As a result, Alexa influenced Francine to become more involved in a worthy cause.

Facing the Possibility of "Failure"

Diana's outward appearance seemed to be a smart young person who was self-assured and very opinionated, yet quite content to hang out with friends and discuss whatever comes to mind. Failure didn't seem to concern her overmuch. When Patricia tried to be available to talk in more depth, Diana became more defensive and put her mother off with "typical" statements ("Let me live my life, Mom!") that Patricia found hurtful. She felt Diana was locking her out. I encouraged Patricia to be patient and continue her positive efforts to be available, yet non-coercive. After years of being a kind of "cheerleader"—building Diana's self-esteem, being positive, and sheltering and nurturing her—I was asking Patricia to challenge her. She found it difficult. I explained how important it is to provide a parental relationship and family environment that challenges teens.

As I said in Chapter 2: "Character Strengths are needed for long-term success. Character Strengths are a reflection of a teen's environment. Character Strengths are a product of teens being consistently encouraged and supported in accepting reasonable risk and challenge. . . . *What's needed is a consistent environment that encourages and supports your teen in accepting reasonable challenges.*"

Patricia didn't really want to hear this. It was a complete change of role for her. And it required her to develop new skills herself. "How do you change the nature of your long-term relationship with your kid?" she asked. I explained that it was a change, but not a complete change. I noted that part of her relationship with Diana was always letting her take on more tasks as she became older. Now that she was on the cusp of adulthood, it was simply a continuation of this process to let go and allow her true Autonomy.

Patricia feared most of all that Diana would continue to get poor grades in her last two years of high school and sabotage her future.

Diana, like many Identity-Building Teens, did not admit to fear of anything. Yet, she avoided taking academic risks regularly. I pointed out that kids from affluent families, like Diana, would delay and avoid tackling situations that could lead to failure. If Diana never applied herself, she could protect herself from failures since she never really tried. I pointed out that Patricia's role was to gently and skillfully open this discussion with her daughter, despite her defensiveness around the issue. Patricia agreed this was important.

I reviewed the principles of Motivational Interviewing with Patricia. At the next session, she shared her attempt at starting the ball rolling in a positive direction with Diana:

Patricia: So, what are your personal goals this semester?
Diana: I'm gonna take it easy this semester and stick with basic classes.
Patricia: So, you feel like just taking it easy.
Diana: Yeah. I'm just gonna chill this semester.
Patricia: You feel like you've worked hard, and you need a break from the pressure of the advanced classes you took last semester.
Diana: Well, yeah. It's not really pressure. I just wanna hang out with my friends a bit more, and I can't do that if I'm studying my head off all the time.
Patricia: It's important to make time to spend with friends.
Diana: Oh yeah. My friends study too much, too, and we end up never seeing one another except at school and online. Every weekend, it's the same. That's it.
Patricia: You really want to set up some fun time with your friends for a change. But they all have some challenging classes, too.
Diana: Yeah. Actually, if I don't take at least one Advanced Placement class, I may not see them much at school.
Patricia: So, maybe selecting one AP class is a good idea.
Diana: Yeah. Maybe one. I dunno.

Patricia: How do you decide?

Diana: I think I'll take AP Biology. It's the most interesting, and Hannah and Liz are gonna be in it.

Patricia didn't tell Diana to take challenging classes, stripping her of her Autonomy, but she did help Diana recognize for herself the consequences of taking the easy classes—in this case, not seeing her friends. By asking open, non-judgmental questions, Patricia removed any assumed pressure of competition by letting Diana choose for herself how she'd handle the upcoming semester.

Lack of motivation is not the base problem for Diana or most Identity-Building Teens; for many teens, it is the lack of accountability. Helicopter Parents, or so-called Tiger Moms, can remove accountability if they attempt to prevent failure at all costs. It can be a tough judgment call on when to hang back and refrain from intervention.

Pressure

For many teens, going back to school means going back to pressure. They see social media and, sometimes, their own high achieving families and decide to drop out of the heated competition early. They look at Advanced Placement courses, GATE (Gifted and Talented Education) courses, and GPA pressures. Who needs it? They'd rather watch television, play video games, surf social media, and spend time with friends. Or they take on low-pressure opportunities like volunteering for something that is important to them, as Diana did with Greenpeace. Most do the minimum required to pass in school. Some miscalculate. If they receive even one C, their chances of getting into the college of their (and their parents') choice greatly diminishes.

Autonomy is about your teen's freedom to make their own decisions and to live with the consequences—even if this means failure. Many parents are not prepared to let this happen. The stakes are too high: it's nothing less than their teen's entire future. How can a parent sit

---

The Struggle Between Mothers and Daughters

"Mothers and daughters struggle in ways that differ from mother–son conflicts or father–son conflicts, which have their own masculine mystery. Mothers and daughters fight more than any other parent–child pair, quarreling twice as much as mothers and sons. One study documented the staying power of mother–daughter sparring: Compared to mother–son arguments, which tend to last about six minutes, mothers and daughters stay engaged for about fifteen minutes.

Even calm, cool, and collected moms will occasionally lose it and get into skirmishes with their frenzied daughters. Despite how irrational they may seem, conflicts between mothers and daughters aren't struggles over nonsense. Very often, low-boil squabbling serves an important function. Going after Mom is a girl's bid to individuate and gain recognition as a different, competent, and unique person. Through bickering, girls can affirm that they are separate selves, and the more exaggerated the conflict, the greater the assurance that 'I'm not anything like my mom.'

Fighting is not necessarily a measure of a bad relationship between a mom and daughter. Moms can be very hurt by what comes across as a form of rejection, but when surveyed later, many girls who quarreled regularly with their moms say they have a close, supportive, and valued relationship. In other words, daughters are spoiling for a fight in order to separate, but they still want the connection."

Source: Kastner, L., & Wyatt, J. (2009). *Getting to calm: Cool-headed strategies for parenting tweens + teens.* Seattle: ParentMap.

---

by and watch a train wreck? Some so-called helicopter parents hover so closely that their teen's motivation is lost in the downdraft. Yet, it's truly a judgment call on how helpful to be versus when to let go.

Whether or not they show it, teens feel the pressure of potential failure. These teens also feel the pressure of figuring out their place *before* they fail too spectacularly to achieve their goals. If you add parental pressure on top of all of the stress they are already feeling, you are depriving your Identity-Building Teen with a secure foothold that they need in establishing their own sense of identity.

Connection Response

I have certainly found that asking too many questions is not a good idea. No one likes to be interrogated. Connection Responses, on the other hand, respect the other person's decision to respond or not. The way in which one listens and offers response matters tremendously. The meta-message (imbedded message) is, hopefully, "I offer this best-guess about what you may be feeling and thinking as a way to show my love and support, not because I require you to respond in this way or that." Remember that your teen may choose not to respond.

Listen with real and accurate empathy, allowing your teen to make their own decisions, rather than forcing your agenda. Remember, this type of teen is searching for and trying out different identities. Expect sudden changes in ideas. When these teens immerse themselves in asking their own questions and generating their own answers, they can become intensely focused and motivated.

My Family's Experience

My kids have shared that their parents are therapists with friends and have gotten comments like, "OMG, I can't believe *both* of your parents are 'shrinks.' I bet they analyze you all the time!" They tell me they just shrug and say, "Nah, not really." Shelley and I are careful not to analyze our kids' thoughts when they tell us how they feel about something that happened during their day. Most of the time, it just feels good to share your feelings and know someone else understands.

Sometimes, however, if one of my kids shares something that reminds me of a memory or strikes me as something they have been struggling with a while, I will say something along the lines of what I am honestly thinking ("You have been thinking about this a long time," or "I remember when you had a very similar situation"). It can help your teen to reflect upon and process a feeling that is a part of an important or recurrent issue they are grappling with. I'm not "the All-Father" (like Odin in the *Thor* comic books) as my son Dylan likes to tease me. Any wisdom I can impart is very limited. But I think it's greatly appreciated when our insights as parents are shared sincerely and in an open-handed way.

I don't expect my advice or insights to necessarily be taken up or even taken seriously. But I offer any insight up in a spirit of hoping my kids would either honestly appreciate my observation or—even better—correct my viewpoint by telling me, "No, I think it's more like this . . ." and go on to disclose more of what they may be thinking. After all, being close to the people you love means, to me, to offer support when they need it most. I just want to be available and do my best as a parent. I want to give my children the tools that they need to connect the dots themselves.

I see that my job as a parent isn't over, even though my kids are all over age eighteen now. Someday I suppose I will be a grandparent, and I will be privileged to give my grandkids whatever love, caring, and support I have to offer.

100 Percent Responsibility Rule

Assist the Identity-Building Teen with the struggle of achieving her vision. This may include listening to her in a supportive manner and helping her to explore options for goal setting and planning. As like in the dialogue example, asking questions can help both of you recognize what it would take to get where they want to go. And when your teen realizes that doing poorly in school or in other areas doesn't help them achieve their goals, it's easier for them to make it a priority.

But even if your teen doesn't come to the conclusions you have, do not become preoccupied with asserting or defending your position or opinion. Avoid becoming highly critical of the Identity-Building Teen.

Remember the 100 Percent Responsibility Rule: "Take all of your responsibility in a given situation, and take none of the teen's responsibility." Since the Identity-Building Teen will eventually find his or her way, it is best to facilitate the process rather than attempt to take over. Do nothing to take responsibility for anything other than doing your job as a parent. The rest is up to them. And your job is just to help your teen connect the dots for how general success is relevant to his or her own goals!

As I have noted, Connection Responses have two parts. One part includes nonjudgmental, non-controlling, empathetic listening combined with reflective statements to let the teen know you have heard and understood her feelings, such as "It sounds like you feel [mad, sad, concerned, etc.] about that," or "I bet you are [disappointed, angry, sad] about that . . ." The second part may include an interpretation or an insight into the underlying issue, memory, or struggle present ("'Think Globally, Act Locally,' right? Let's set one concrete thing we can do locally and get it done so . . ." or "That sounds admirable. What do you need to do to get there?"). As I have observed, sometimes it's better not to read too much into any one statement your teen makes. No need to analyze every sentence.

My Family's Experience

I understand the dilemma that parents face. My daughter Claire was placed in an advanced math class in high school. It turned out in this class the textbook was faulty, and Claire tried pointing out the error to the teacher after a test came back with poor marks. The teacher was intransient and the two clashed over the disagreement. Claire was at risk of failing the class, and the teacher wouldn't work with us. Shelley and I set up a conference to advocate with the school to arrange a transfer out of the class before the first grading period ended. We even brought in Shelley's father, who is a mathematician and who's taught on the undergraduate and graduate level.

We were successful in transferring Claire—which we look back on as a turning point, since even one poor grade could have torpedoed her application to get into the University of California. I tell the story to illustrate the real dilemma parents face: When do you advocate and when do you let go? I think the decision can be made by applying the 100 Percent Responsibility Rule. What part of this is my responsibility as a parent and what part is my teen's responsibility? The advocacy role was clearly up to me and Shelley (with her dad's help). After that, it was up to Claire to apply herself in a more appropriate math class.

Emma and Her Parents

Emma, a sixteen-year-old eleventh grader, sat at her usual place during her nightly homework time. She wanted to be a research scientist and cure diseases. Emma read widely about progress in the area of new psychiatric medications and joined websites, such as Journal Watch and Research Gate, to keep abreast of changes in the field. She applied for a summer internship at a local research facility. But while she was doing really well in her science classes, she didn't seem at all interested or invested in history or English courses.

One night, she had her desk chair turned toward her large Mac monitor and was watching her fifth dance video. She shoved her chair aside and mimicked the sequence of dance moves she saw in the video. Her mother, Denise, peeked in and saw her dance moves. She turned around to look at Emma's dad, Mitch. She was exasperated with Emma and said, "It's your turn. Somehow get her back to her work! I can't do it anymore."

"Emma, it's late! Get back to your homework!" he yelled. Emma opened her history textbook, but within ten minutes, was cueing up another dance video.

Emma and her parents were locked in a kind of pointless battle. The key, I explained to Denise and Mitch, is figuring out how to get

Emma to tune into her own motivation and for them to get out of the role of shielding her from failure and disappointment.

As I spoke with Denise and Mitch, I understood that they had spent a lot of time and effort to ensure Emma had good self-esteem. I complimented them on their efforts. I also reviewed the research on Autonomy, Competence, and Relatedness as factors in the service of developing Character Strengths—particularly the ability to persevere in the face of difficulty and failure (also known as Grit).

This was a bridge too far for Denise and Mitch. They explained that failure was not an option for Emma. She was smart and *had* to go to a good college. She would not be accepted at a good college if she did poorly in even one class. I explained that for Emma to learn to deal with failure was a life lesson she would need to face sooner or later.

I went into some detail about why dealing with and overcoming failure was so important. Denise and Mitch had to make the same shift in thinking that Patricia did. It required them to let go of control and possibly be witnesses to minor and maybe even major train wrecks. Emma could get a C, D, or even an F for missing assignments. Yet I explained how important it was for Emma to face the consequences of her own actions.

As the semester progressed, Emma failed to turn in a major assignment on time. She was utterly demoralized. The next week, she did the same thing in yet another class. She expected her parents to intervene and call the teacher to ask for an extension. Denise and Mitch did not make the call as Emma had asked. This time, Emma got mad.

"This sucks, and it is your fault!" she yelled.

She was called into the academic counselor's office and asked to account for the drop in her grades. The counselor told her she would be placed in two lower-level courses as a result.

Emma remained angry at her parents for "not caring" about her. But because she did not want to be placed into the lower-level classes, she filed an appeal. For the first time, she considered that she may not get into a good college, which is what Denise and Mitch had been telling her for a long time. When Emma was told she had to spend at least one semester in the two lower-level classes, Denise and Mitch were really worried she would become overwhelmed or even depressed.

Since Emma was used to being rescued by her parents, she was confused. She waited to see if they would take some kind of action. Eventually, she came up with the idea of asking her teachers for help. Fortunately, they were both willing to help, but only if she made the appointments herself and came consistently. In these meetings, Emma learned her honors science and advanced math teachers had both failed classes in college that they had to retake. One of her teachers told her if she did not take responsibility for her own learning, she should give up on the idea of being a science major in college. Emma was shaken by this blunt statement, since she was counting on this teacher to give her a strong recommendation. She continued to show up for her appointments and began to make solid academic progress.

Appropriate Challenge

Diana and Emma, like so many teens, had become accustomed to being praised, sheltered, and protected over the years by well-intentioned parents. We all know the Little League and soccer "trophies" kids get for just showing up. Teens also know, as they approach adulthood, that the world just doesn't work that way. No one gets a trophy for just showing up. Research has found that continuously telling kids they are good at something can actually discourage them from trying harder.

Requiring more, not less, from teens is a good thing. Remember, Authoritative Parents are *both* very supportive and very demanding. Chores and responsibilities around the house should be expected. Treating teens like royalty who are to bring honor to the family gives them an unrealistic message. Seeing a parent take out the garbage does not inspire a teen to rush, with gratitude, to their studies. Rather, she may draw the conclusion "I am above all of that." Successful people are the ones who are willing to do things that they don't want to do.[4] Setting effective limits is also a part of Authoritative Parenting. The rules of the world *do* apply!

Finally, make sure the challenges you issue as a parent are reasonable ones. The aim is parental authority as a service, for your teen's benefit and not as a feather in your cap. Provide consistent support to face reasonable challenges ("What's needed is a consistent environment that encourages and supports your teen in accepting reasonable challenges," from chapter 2). Perhaps your teen doesn't want to go to a four-year college. A community college could be a better choice. One college counselor put it this way: "A good college is the one that fits your kid, not whose name adds class to your car's rear window."

Key Action Steps ✓

- Use Connection Responses frequently to build feelings of Relatedness, Autonomy, and Competence. Remember, when an Identity-Building Teen feels your judgment, they lose a secure foothold on their identity and can feel more lost.
- The Identity-Building Teen needs help connecting the dots on how their current academic success is relevant to their goals. Help them with that self-discovery rather than just imposing your own ideas on them.
- Use the 100 Percent Responsibility Rule to know when to advocate for your teen, but don't prevent them from learning the consequences of their actions—even if they fail.
- Provide challenge and open communication for your teen at home.
- Be patient and recognize that the Identity-Building Teen *will* grow out of any under-achieving habits as they find their direction.

CHAPTER 8

The Trust-Building Teen

S ofia is a Trust-Building Teen. In elementary school, she did very well. She was near the top of her class. She finished her work before most of the other students. She enjoyed helping peers and created a winning project at the science fair. But when she turned seventeen her life completely changed after her parents divorced. She moved to a new neighborhood and hung around with an entirely different set of friends. Her mother, Jocelyn, had taken on a second job as a newly single parent, so she was not around in the afternoon when Sofia and her brothers got out of school. Sofia was then required to be in the apartment with her brothers until her mom got home. But as soon as her mom did get home, Sofia often left to go out with friends. She stayed out late even on weeknights.

With her added responsibilities concerning her siblings, her habit of staying out late, and her heightened stress, Sofia often arrived late to school and would fall asleep during class. As Sofia's grades dropped, she lost interest in academics.

When a teen has been exposed to chronic stress, their academic work—and other aspects of their lives—are usually profoundly affected.

Chronic Anxiety

There are times when there are good reasons for teens to feel anxious. If there's been domestic violence; verbal, physical or sexual abuse; addiction; divorce; or any other extremely stressful event in the family, a teen will naturally feel anxious and insecure, even within their own home. If the neighborhood isn't safe, anxiety is a natural reaction to the dangerous circumstances. News stories about terrorism, disaster, or crime can exacerbate the sense of insecurity a teen experiencing chronic anxiety feels.

Research has demonstrated that teens are especially vulnerable to the effects of chronic stress.[1] Adolescence is a time of many social, emotional, and physiological changes, including stress-related hormonal responses. The still-maturing teen brain contributes to and, indeed, amplifies stress-related issues including anxiety and depression.[2]

If a divorce, alcoholism/addiction in the family, economic setbacks, or other chronic stress play a role, it is important to get outside support for yourself and your teen. Short- or long-term professional counseling can be very helpful. Sometimes it is offered as part of school services.

Research on Chronic Stress

A well-known ACES research study reveals the toll stress and trauma can take on teens. ACES stands for Adverse Childhood Experiences. Robert Anda, a doctor at the Centers for Disease Control, and Vincent Felitti, a doctor at Kaiser Permanente, conducted a study of seventeen thousand Kaiser patients. They identified ten categories of stressful situations (including divorce, family violence, mental illness, addiction, and incarceration of a parent). They found that adults who had experienced four or more of these situations in their families had much higher chance of having serious medical issues, including cancer, and heart, liver, and lung disease, as well as higher rates of depression, anxiety, suicide, and self-destructive behaviors. But the ACES criteria were most effective for identifying chronic stress in kids' lives and its long-term effect.

A teen who experiences significant stress may find the only recourse to express their frustration, anger, or sadness is in their behavior. If the teen feels overwhelmed by the stress or is angry with his parents, resistance may assume the form of aggressiveness or rebellion, such as refusing to do chores or homework assignments. Chronic stress has a myriad of other more serious long-term effects as well.

Stress comes in many forms. Most teens have seen many of the stressful realities of life, yet do not fully understand them. They may have experienced the death of a family member or a friend. Many teens experience rejection, fear, defeat, disappointment, and disillusionment even more intensely than adults do because all of these experiences are new to them. Yet, their view of the world and understanding of cause and effect are still developing.

Your teen's developing ability to deal with stress is ongoing, even at a neurological level. Contrary to conventional wisdom, recent research has shown the adolescent brain continues to develop in ways every bit as important as early childhood, before age three: "The last area of the brain to be hooked up . . . is the prefrontal cortex, which controls insight, judgment, self-awareness, and empathy—the brain's so-called 'executive' functions."[3] As we observed in chapter 1, the executive function of the brain is the way neuroscientists talk about the way teens develop the soft skills—the Character Strengths—needed to cope with stress and reach success in academics and in life.

If a teenager experiences intense stressors—as Sofia did with the divorce of her parents—their sense of stability and trust is significantly compromised.

What Can a Parent Do?

Fortunately, there are important and effective ways a parent can mitigate the effects of chronic stress. The family environment matters—that is, the way a parent and other adults in their lives interact with them—especially in times of stress.

Addressing the Trust-Building Teen's emotional needs is important. The Trust-Building Teen is sometimes described as the behavioral result of an emotional "perfect storm" when students are struggling to deal with family issues, school challenges, and personal difficulties. A Trust-Building Teen may shift academics to the backburner and lose motivation and self-confidence.

These factors can be difficult to predict or prevent. Many lay outside of the parents' control. Despite our best efforts, changes in life circumstances come along and may become very disruptive in the student's life. Even though serious stressors may be present in their life, research shows kids will respond very favorably to comfort and support given at the precise times when they are most distressed.

Critical Moments

Is there anything you can do, as a parent, to help compensate for the effect of chronic stress?

Research has shown that parents who behave erratically or unpredictably when their kids are very upset and stressed can have a serious and long-term negative impact on their ability to handle stress.[4] Think about it; not only is your teen learning how to handle (or not handle) stressful situations by watching you, they are also experiencing the "fight, flight, or freeze" feelings of anxiety—the sinking feeling in the pit of your stomach—that we all feel at stressful times.

The good news is that parents who are able to help their kids at these times may see a profound and lasting positive impact. In response to stress, teens can be disorganized, unable to pay attention to their environment, and neglectful of their homework assignments.

They can be just as surprised as you are by their unpredictable behavior and their uneven response to stress.[5] Teens learn to calm themselves down after upsetting experiences, often with the help of an adult or parent. You can model and teach your teen how to identify what they are feeling and how to process their emotions in healthy ways. This can have a profoundly positive effect on their long-term ability to learn to manage stress.

So you, as a parent, have a lot of influence in helping your teen through chronic and acutely stressful situations.

When parents provide a timely, soothing response to anxiety and stress, teens are more likely to develop the ability to cope successfully with anxiety in the future—even in very stressful situations. Some coping or moderating tactics include exercise and getting enough rest. And the most helpful communication skill to use with a Trust-Building Teen is the Connection Response.

The Connection Response

As always, the Connection Response is a primary way to help your teen. The Connection Response requires a parent to be a good listener, acknowledge the feeling that underlies their teen's words, and help the teen identify what they are feeling.

Being a good listener means focusing attention on your teen when they need it most. Your care and attention can have a most healing effect, especially when your teen is feeling overwhelmed.

Be an active listener; connect by making eye contact, turn off the television, and make sure that there is no outside interference. By keeping the lines of conversation open, your teen will be more likely to open up to you when they feel most stressed. Take the opportunity exactly when they are willing to talk and disclose their innermost feelings. Such times can arise unexpectedly, but be ready.

As much as is possible, spend individual time each day with your teen. Plan an individual outing with your teen at least once a week, even if it is short like going to McDonald's for a vanilla ice cream cone or to 7-Eleven for a Slurpee. During the individual time, try not to ask too many questions. On the outing, just have a good time with your teen. Share your positive thoughts and feelings. Let your teen know you value your relationship with them.

Hopefully, with this pattern of open communication in place, your teen will trust that they can share all their feelings and reactions without fear of punishment or criticism. Body language, voice level, and words can be as low-key and non-judgmental as possible. This will help your teen concentrate on how they are feeling.

If you are too overpowering, it will tend to make them more aware of *your* thoughts and feelings, not their own. In response, they will tend to become more anxious. Or, conversely, a Trust-Building Teen may withdraw and become distrustful of all adults. Remember that the Trust-Building Teen is still developing their ability to discern their own thoughts and feelings to begin with. You, as a parent, are most often in the best place to help your teen overcome the effects of chronic stress. Even if your relationship is strained or seemingly broken down, you are the one best able to help your teen learn the all-important skills of how to use self-calming and relaxation when they need them most. Teens' response to stress can go haywire easily. Research shows teens from ages eleven to fifteen become sad and anxious when subjected to social stress, including exclusion from social groups. Parts of their brain most vulnerable to stress are still maturing. Researchers advise teaching and modeling self-soothing skills, such as meditation, exercise, or listening to music. In older teens, executive function skills are continuing to develop at least through age twenty.[6]

The 100 Percent Responsibility Rule

Remember that the rule is simply this: "Take 100 percent of your own responsibility; take zero percent of theirs." Although you have no absolute control over your teen, their behavior, or outside circumstances, it is important to remember that you still have tremendous influence as a parent.

For some typical situations for Trust-Building Teens, this rule becomes a little trickier. When Sofia's parents divorced, it precipitated some dramatic changes to her life and stress level. It is certainly true that Sofia's mom, Jocelyn, had the responsibility to talk through the changes with her children and help them find healthy ways to adjust to all of the changes, it was *not* her job to dictate how Sofia spends her time, which friends she makes, or how to feel about all of the changes that have happened to her and the family.

So, how can you use your limited influence to help the Trust-Building Teen?

Parents provide support, but the art of balancing how much support to provide and exactly when to withdraw support is important. Your teen needs to face reasonable challenges regularly to develop Character Strengths, as we observed early on. If your teen detects that you are trying to be overly directive, controlling, or just too helpful, your approach is likely to be counterproductive.

The art of withdrawing support at the right time is related to your teen developing a sense of Competence as well. Teens are very sensitive to their emerging identity, reputation, and sense of being admired and valued.[7] If an adult comes in and has to tell the teen what to do, it tends to makes them feel less Competent.

For teens, feeling the sense of accomplishment and Competence is tremendously valuable. "Catch 'em being good" is a great motto with younger kids. As your teen becomes older, more self-aware, and independent, it's helpful to modify the motto to "Catch 'em taking a positive step and admire it!" If your teen is going in an unhelpful direction, it's better to step back and—if no permanent damage will be done—let them learn on their own. If you try to intervene too much, you'll lose 'em.

Detachment from that which is beyond your control is the all-important attitude that differentiates between what you are responsible for and what you are not, what you have the power to control and what you do not. Accepting full responsibility for your actions as a parent implies you will act to the best of your ability in any given situation and refrain from attempting to coerce the teen's decisions, emotions, or actions.

With regard to parenting decisions, this involves focus on the behavior rather than the attitude of your son or daughter. Setting behavioral expectations is helpful, but since you have no absolute control, you will need to be flexible. You may need to try quite a few suggestions and approaches. Remember to use the "soft power" of persuasion, support, and listening along with the "hard power" of rules and requirements.

With some difficulty, Jocelyn realized she needed to accept some outside help for the family. She decided she had begun to rely on Sofia too much for childcare. After enrolling her two younger sons in the afterschool childcare assistance program, she apologized to Sofia for relying on her help too often to watch her younger brothers. At the same time, she set a rule about not staying out past eight p.m. on school nights. She knew Sofia wouldn't like this "hard power" rule, but she felt it was her responsibility to set this expectation.

Jocelyn also accepted a school counselor referral for Sofia to attend in-school counseling and a mentoring program. Sofia went to the counseling even though she didn't want to attend at first. Sofia's mentor, Kelly, was a student from a local community college. Sofia and Kelly got along really well. Over the next few months, Sofia began to do better in school again with Kelly's encouragement. At the same time, Sofia accepted help in counseling to learn some stress-reduction "tricks," including how to use Mindfulness Meditation to relax. Jocelyn noted that her communication with Sofia improved a lot. Jocelyn came to see that Sofia had let go of her anger and stress about the big changes in her life after the divorce. Jocelyn felt that Sofia had finally forgiven her.

My Family's Experience

Shelley and I worked hard to help our kids establish habits to manage stress. Shelley never participated in a sport when she was growing up, so she really wanted our kids to be involved. She found that, as an adult, she was less confident when she was invited to go kayaking or to try a new sports activity. We decided to strongly encourage our kids to take up a sports activity. That was the solid Right Hand, "hard power" part. The Left Hand, "soft power" part, involved the choice. The particular sport to be involved with was up to each of our kids individually. That provided the Autonomy. Once again, I make it sound easy. In reality, each of our kids, being individuals, responded quite differently. Team sports like soccer and Little League were a part of the mix. Sometimes just going on a walk together was the activity.

Trust-Building Teens need specific concrete strategies to cope with stress—the "fight, flight, or freeze" feelings everyone experiences—but Trust Builders experience stress even more intensively because of their ACES. Exercise is one of the best ways to manage stress. Encourage your teen to sign up for sports. Team sports are a great way to meet peers and exercise, but some teens would prefer solo activities. That's OK. Yoga, swimming, surfing, running, biking, walking, and hiking are all forms of exercise that can become a life-long positive pastime. Set an example by inviting your teen along for an active outing. See if you can keep up with your teen!

Getting enough sleep is important, too. Stressed teens often have sleep problems. It can become a vicious cycle. Sleep loss problems for teens are linked with emotional, behavioral, and mental health issues.[8] When teens don't get enough sleep, they tend to become irritable and stress tends to increase. Conversely, getting enough sleep can be healing and the best way to make a new start. Setting limits on smartphone, computer, video games, and television may be necessary, especially in the evening.

You can teach your teen time-management skills. I personally like the positive habit of making lists and prioritizing the items on my list as one circle, two circles, or three circles. This method is featured in many "how to" books, including *How to Get Control of Your Time and Your Life* by Alan Lakein. When I write something down, it gets it off my mind. When I get an item done, I get to check it off. The check-off feels good and relieves the stress of having the task hanging out there.

Of course, all this depends on your teen's individual personality. They may use your great suggestions and techniques immediately. Or (more likely) they may have their own ideas. Brainstorming different ways to organize and then letting go so they can make their own decision is key. Don't forget to let go. Sometimes, you will find one of your suggestions is discarded immediately, only to return days, weeks, or months later when your teen tells you they thought of it themselves.

Supportive School Programs

I was a founding staff member in a school program designed to help students who needed extra support. This is particularly for students in high-risk situations. In this capacity, I saw the need and response of many kids who needed that extra support. DeAndre was a tenth grader in the non-public school alternative program, for which I served as school psychologist. He told me he liked me because of my last name. He said his uncle was a founder of the Gangster Disciples in Chicago and that they had made it a point to study the methods of Lucky Luciano and the Mafia, hence the name "Disciples." I told DeAndre I am not related to Lucky Luciano, but he said he still liked me even though I am not a relative of the famous gangster.

I had no idea whether what DeAndre told me was true or not, but I recognized his outreach to me in a new school was his way of increasing Relatedness, as Deci and Ryan defined it. He challenged me to a push-up contest in the school yard. I was game and managed to keep up with him for a while. Once, he lunged at me unexpectedly, coming an inch from my face. I laughed and looked at him with a quizzical expression. I think he did this to test me and his own sense of increasing status—to see if he could be intimidating and whether I would flinch. In this rather unusual way, DeAndre attempted to build his sense of self-esteem and Competence.

DeAndre spent a semester in the smaller and more restrictive environment of the alternative school program. He made some academic progress and didn't get into any trouble, but I think the real progress he made involved his relationships with the staff. He wasn't involved in gang activity (as far as I knew), despite his talk. It appeared to me that he had benefitted from the smaller class size and the increased attention from caring professionals in the program; that is, he benefitted from the increased sense of Relatedness, Competence, and Autonomy a smaller school and class size can sometimes provide.

The smaller, specialized program was designed to address Trust-Building Teens' needs. Their teachers played a crucial role. All educators must balance the responsibilities of four main objectives: provide content knowledge; set up appropriate academic challenges (at the correct instructional level); actively teach organizational skills; and note any indications of mental, emotional, or psychological unease. Identifying and addressing any issues is important before the student gets further behind academically.

As teens begin to ask questions about their place in the world and the stability of that place, they will need emotionally reliable teachers with high expectations to help them set up their goals. School and other professional counselors may play a crucial role since many Trust-Building Teens face emotional challenge, difficult life circumstances, and other personal challenges.

Advocacy

Learning disabilities, ADHD, or even a mismatch between students' learning style and teachers' preferred style of instruction can be significant factors in the school setting. In some situations, it is important for a parent to intervene as their teen's advocate with the school district. If your teen has an Individualized Education Plan (IEP) or if they go to an underperforming school as identified in the federal *Every Student Succeeds Act* (2015), there may be steps you can take under the law to actively advocate and intervene for them with the school administration. You could obtain more professional services or change to a more appropriate school program as a result.

Seeking Extra Support

The Trust-Building Teen may have low self-esteem and experience feelings of depression and sadness. Often, they lack the energy to concentrate on school work and may be too fatigued to motivate themselves to achieve. It is important to find out the underlying issue behind the depression.

Some teens handle criticism and disapproval better than others. Their response can provide insight into their personality. Moreover, if the depression and anxiety is due to a stressor, such as an alcoholic parent, parents' divorce, any abuse, or traumatic stress, the issue must be addressed before the Trust-Building Teen will improve.

Professional counseling may be needed to address the teen's depression or anxiety and to help him or her to develop coping skills. Remember, a teen may not admit to feelings of sadness or anxiety, but the hidden feelings may show up as behavioral or academic problems.

Key Action Steps ✔

- It's best to approach the Trust-Building Teen in a supportive manner. It is important not to add to their underlying anxiety and stress.
- As always, look into the issues behind the teen's behavior. Make Connection Responses to share your best guesses about how they

are doing. Don't give up even if there appears to be no response.

- Model and help your teen to use ways to reduce tension and stress, especially when they are most upset by stressors. Encourage them to learn and use stress management, relaxation, meditation, slow breathing, and mindfulness if they are open to learning them.

- Maintain the 100 Percent Responsibility Rule by recognizing your job of providing stability for your teen despite stressful circumstances and giving emotional support when they come to you. Do not take on responsibility for any acting out or failure to perform in school.

- Be approachable when the Trust-Building Teen needs you the most. Be genuine and willing to give honest and straightforward feedback in a gentle, but assertive way ("You know, I'm concerned about what you did").

- Assist them in making their own homework schedule. Include a plan for organizing their time and encourage independence once a schedule has been determined.

- Use a simple checklist system. Keep it short with just two or three items. When these items are accomplished, declare the day a success.

- Gently provide logical, supportive responses to their negative beliefs ("Just because you didn't get the grade you wanted doesn't mean you are [stupid, a loser, etc.]").

- Give genuine praise when you see extra effort. Be careful with any feedback that could be taken as criticism.

- After you give feedback, use a Connection Response to check if they interpreted what said as you intended.

CHAPTER 9

Bottom Line

We have seen that Character Strengths as grit, self-control, zest, social intelligence, gratitude, optimism, and curiosity are a necessary condition for teens' long-term success. The best way for teens to build Character Strengths is to tackle challenges regularly—and be willing to accept and overcome failure along the way. Parents who consistently encourage and support their teen in accepting reasonable risk and challenge are most apt to help them develop these Character Strengths.

Which brings us back to the question this book is attempting to answer: What happens when your teen avoids challenging situations?

The situation is complex and rather tricky when a teen has developed a habitual aversion to accepting reasonable risk and challenge, when they have become Challenge Averse.

We have examined a wide range of insights into intervening with such teens. Character Strengths cannot be directly taught as academic subjects can; these traits must be fostered and encouraged over time in the family and school environments. Fortunately, many researchers have identified reliable methods to develop Character Strengths as a reflection of the family environment and the parents' relationship with their teen.

The task is to develop a consistent environment that encourages and supports teens in accepting reasonable challenges. Not too much risk and challenge, not too little; the "Goldilocks Zone."

The Authoritative Parenting Style

As we have seen, the Authoritative Parenting style is the one most associated with positive outcomes in the research. It's part of the answer. Authoritative Parents provide high levels of both behavioral limits and parental support. They set high behavioral requirements, while simultaneously providing a nurturing and responsive family environment. They respect teens as independent and able to make decisions.

Authoritative Parenting can be challenging. To be sure, it requires being selective about when to intervene, being available and aware of your teen's behavior without hovering, and being realistic about the fact that teens are not perfectly compliant.

Behavioral limits and parental support are equally important.

The Three Essential Conditions and Intrinsic Motivation

We have seen that researchers Edward Deci and Richard Ryan iden-tified three essential conditions to encourage intrinsic motivation:

Relatedness, Autonomy, and Competence. Teens feel a sense of Relatedness when they perceive that their parents like, value, and respect them. They experience Autonomy when their parents emphasize a sense of choice while minimizing feelings of coercion and control. And they feel Competent when their parents give them tasks that they can succeed at, but are not too easy—reasonable challenges just beyond their current abilities.

When these three conditions are met, teens are able to develop a personal sense of motivation that goes beyond obedience or fear of consequences. They are more ambitious and confident in their abilities.

The Connection Response

The communication skill that we use most often with teens is the Connection Response. Recall, it both acknowledges the feeling that underlies words and encourages the connection of other situations when the teen may have felt the same way. It may start with reflective listening and restating your teen's thoughts and feelings ("Looks like that made you feel [mad, sad, overwhelmed, etc.]"). In doing this, you seek to clarify the feeling content *and* encourage more insight.

The Connection Response helps your teen to connect the dots between feelings and reactions on their own, though with your guidance as an active listener.

As we observed, being a good listener means focusing attention on your teen and refraining from formulating an answer before they have finished speaking. It also requires removing distractions like phones or television. Teens are especially good at detecting whether a parent or teacher is really listening or is simply waiting to continue talking (or lecturing). As a parent, you can be a model for becoming a good listener. In most situations, modeling is the most powerful way to teach non-cognitive skills.

The 100 Percent Responsibility Rule

The rule is simple, but the application is nuanced. Recall the 100 Percent Responsibility Rule is "Take all of your responsibility, take zero percent of theirs." In the realm of parenting a Challenge-Averse Teen, the application of the rule can be complex. The questions are "What is my responsibility as a parent in this situation?" and "What is my teen's responsibility?" The answer depends on a number of factors.

Most importantly, take into account your teen's current abilities. Can they do this on their own? How much help do they need? The general principle here is "If they can do it, don't do it for them." Why? It is part of presenting the Goldilocks Zone challenges—not too difficult, not too easy. As all parents know, teens (and all of us) are learning all the time.

If they can't do something on their own or if they need your advocacy, how much do you need to handle before they can accomplish their responsibility?

Allow me to leave you with one more story about applying these ideas in a practical way.

Daniel and His Parents

Daniel was staying up late playing video games, watching internet videos, and chatting with Facebook friends. He was able to get up in the morning to go to school at the community college, but obviously felt tired and fatigued later in the day. Since attempting to enforce a bedtime or taking away the game console would be futile with a nineteen-year-old, his parents, Sara and David, watched his struggles with increasing alarm. They attempted to explain the importance of a good night's sleep to Daniel, but he ignored their advice. When Sara mentioned she noticed how much time he was spending playing video games, both during the day and in the evening, Daniel seemed to become even more closed-minded about the subject.

Sara and David sought an education consultation. They explained Daniel would not come in for counseling, but they knew they had to take some kind of action since he was on track to fail his remedial community college classes. Although Daniel would not personally come in for a session, I reviewed some of the principles of communication proven to be helpful to influence teens with Sara and David.

With Sara and David, I reviewed Dr. Ron Dahl's specific suggestions1 from the Motivational Interviewing playbook:

1. Make an empathic connection
2. Ask open-ended questions
3. Use reflective listening
4. Use non-confrontational ways to point out inconsistencies
5. Support Autonomy
6. Join Resistance: that is, don't directly disagree with what is said but instead pick out the part you can agree with as much as you can. Emphasize where you agree.
7. Be genuine and value the teen's viewpoint
8. Shift the intensity of the discussion
9. Re-state their opposing viewpoint, and
10. When they are ready, help make a plan of action.

I explained some of the key aspects of Motivational Interviewing that could be helpful. Sara explained that Daniel was able to earn a high school diploma, although it was the lesser of two types of diplomas offered by the San Diego School District. She also explained that Daniel was fully capable of earning the higher diploma, but he had failed two classes in his last year due to his "video game addiction." Sara and David asked me to set up a plan of action to influence Daniel in a positive direction.

I reviewed the research about developing intrinsic motivation with Sara and David. I also explained the three basic elements of Motivational Interviewing—Collaboration, Evocation, and Autonomy—and how they could use these ideas as a practical way to influence Daniel.

Collaboration is very much akin to Relatedness. I explained Collaboration involves fostering an environment in which Daniel understands that they, as parents, like him, respect his viewpoint, and are willing to work with him to help him achieve his goals.

Evocation refers to a parent's use of open-ended questions and reflective listening to help Daniel to identify his internal motivations. Sound familiar? The concept is quite similar to what we have been referring to as the Connection Response: active listening plus an orientation to insight.

Autonomy refers to the teen's responsibility to make the decision whether or not to change his behavior. Autonomy does not mean independence, but rather refers to having a sense of free will when doing something in your own interests. In Motivational Interviewing, Autonomy emphasizes the teen's free will regarding their own behavior. I have been using the idea of 100 percent responsibility as a way to explain and amplify these ideas.

I reviewed ways to implement these concepts with Sara and David.

Empathy was first on the list. Sara and David had tried to simply persuade Daniel that the excessive amount of time he played video games and surfed the internet was harming him. Sara would sit Daniel down for heart-to-heart talks about her feelings about it. David, for his part, tried a logical approach, explaining how habit-forming video games could be. He sent articles on the subject to Daniel in email. He tried to approach the topic when he saw that Daniel had received a poor grade on a test, probably because he had not put in the time to study. He thought that may be a good time to persuade Daniel to give up the video game addiction.

I had Sara and David role play so I could demonstrate using empathic, reflective listening, and Connection Responses. I showed with examples that it was better to listen and reflect the content of what Daniel was saying and also how important it is not to show even nonverbal disapproval or judgment of his behavior.

Reflecting Daniel's viewpoint was hard for both Sara and David since it meant reflecting a view in which they simply did not believe, but rather saw as harmful to Daniel. They quoted Daniel as saying, "I like gaming and a lot of my friends online like it, too. When I play *Call of Duty* online, my friends are all there. It's fun, and it's my generation's way of getting together." It took a monumental effort for Sara and David to rephrase these kinds of statements into Connection Responses and to understand and reflect the feelings behind them because they sincerely believed the activity was poison for their son.

I helped them to scissor out any negative or judgmental parts of their attempts to use reflective listening: "So, playing *Call of Duty* is like getting together with friends for you." Sara couldn't help frowning as she said this. She tried her best to change her expression. She continued, "You get to chat with them online. You even meet people from around the country who like the game. You feel good when you play a long time."

We also practiced Rolling with Resistance. I explained that if Daniel became defensive while discussing his video game playing or internet use, it was important to back away from the topic or even join with any resistance to discussing it by agreeing with his sentiment that video gaming was undoubtedly fun at times.

As consultation progressed over the course of a few months, Sara told me about her conversations with Daniel. She said, surprisingly, Daniel had admitted that he didn't always feel good about playing video games for hours in a row. Sometimes, he admitted, he needed a break. Sara told me she was able to refrain from jumping on the admission and stayed with Connection Responses and reflective listening. She responded with something like, "So, sometimes you feel like you need a break from the electronics."

I suggested adding some open-ended questions ("What is it like when you know you've probably skipped some study time because you got caught up playing online?" and "Is there anything else going on you want to talk about?"). I suggested using the last open-ended question as a way to lighten the discussion and change the subject to something Daniel wanted to talk about.

Daniel wanted his parents to watch some video with him. David ended up watching one of Daniel's favorite shows on Netflix with Daniel, even though he didn't find the black humor in it all that funny. I explained that doing things like that could really be helpful, since teens really like it when they can influence their parents in some way. It builds Relatedness and feelings of Competence. It also showed Daniel that his dad liked spending time with him and respected his viewpoint. It was a part of genuinely appreciating one of Daniel's interests.

After a few months of consultation, Sara and David told me Daniel had decided to delete his Facebook account and he had curtailed his video gaming substantially. One important factor was that he got a job and had made some new friends as a result. Sara and David were glad to see Daniel make "live" friends that he wanted to spend more time with than his internet video gaming and social media friends.

Sara and David had to learn how to implement all of the skills and communication patterns when dealing with Daniel and his challenges. They worked to identify the core causes for his lack of success in school and his preoccupation with his apparent addiction. As they made that effort, their son became prepared to cope with the challenges he was facing in school and real-life situations. Sara noticed a number of good things happening in Daniel's life that she attributed to his increasing confidence. She saw much less tension between Daniel and David. She also observed that Daniel's willingness to face challenges had increased as he felt less criticized and more empowered at home. He was willing to take risks and put himself on the line by interviewing for—and getting—a job as a special education classroom aide. Even more importantly, she saw their relationship with Daniel had improved significantly!

Summing It Up: Simple Things

My martial arts instructor, Master Mique, often said, "Simple things, simple things." He meant that after you learn the basics, it's important to look at the big picture and understand the simplicity of the whole. I hope the information in this book will become a simple thing to you as a parent.

Listen.

Let go.

Have some simple rules.

Give lots of warmth and support.

Build your family life with Confidence, Independence, Initiative, Identity, and Trust.

God bless!

Endnotes

Introduction

1. Desilver, D. (2017). US students' academic achievement still lags behind that of their peers in many countries. *Pew Research Center.* Retrieved from http://www.pewresearch.org/fact-tank/2017/02/15/u-s-students-internationally-math-science/.
2. Chuck, E. (2015, November 18). Just over half of all college students actually graduate, report finds. *NBC News.*
3. Rimm, S. (1995). *Why bright kids get poor grades: And what you can do about it.* New York: Three Rivers Press.
4. ACT. (2016). The condition of college & career readiness 2016.
5. Pew Research Center. (2015, July 29). More millennials living with family despite improved job market.
6. Thompson, T. & Parker, C. (2007, May/June). Fear of failure key to understanding underachieving students. *Educational Research Newsletter, 20(5).*
7. Pecaut, L. S. (1979). *Understanding and influencing student motivation.* Glen Ellyn, IL: Institute for Motivational Development.

Chapter 1

1. Tough, P. (2012). *How children succeed.* New York: Houghton Mifflin Harcourt.
2. Tough, P. (2016). *Helping children succeed.* New York: Houghton Mifflin Harcourt.
3. Hoskins, D. (2014). Consequences of parenting on adolescent outcomes. *Societies* 4(3), 506–531.
4. Baumrind, D. (1966). Effects of authoritative parental control on child behavior. *Child Development* 37(4), 887–907.
5. Ibid.
6. Maccoby, E. E., & Martin, J. A. (1983). Socialization in the context of the family: Parent-child interaction. In P. H. Mussen & E. M. Hetherington (Eds.), *Handbook of child psychology: Vol. 4* (pp. 1–101). New York: Wiley.

Chapter 2

1. Ryan, R. M., & Deci, E. L. (2000). Self-determination theory and the facilitation of intrinsic motivation, social development, and well-being. *American Psychologist* 55(1), 68–78.
2. Tough, P. (2012). *How children succeed.*
3. Heard from Rabbi Harold Kushner; attributed by some to Senator Paul Tsongas.

Chapter 3

1. Erikson, E. (1950). *Childhood and society.* New York: W. W. Norton & Co.

Chapter 4

1. Denizet-Lewis, B. (2017, October 17). Why are more teenagers than ever suffering from severe anxiety? *New York Times Magazine.*
2. Ibid.
3. Zimbardo, P. G. (1997). *Shyness: What it is, what to do about it.* New York: Perseus Books..

Chapter 5

1. Tough, P. (2012). *How children succeed.*
2. Bodenhamer, G. (1983). *Back in control.* Upper Saddle River, NJ: Prentice Hall.
3. Berne, E. (1996). *Games people play: The basic handbook of transactional analysis.* New York: Ballantine. See also Steiner, C. (1984). *Games alcoholics play.* New York: Ballantine.

Chapter 6

1. *Urban Dictionary:* popularized by the *Beavis* and *Butt-head* V series, "dillweed" is a derogatory term used to describe irrational/ dumb behavior and low intellectual capacity, usually resulting in some sort of consequence.
2. Mandel, H. P., & Marcus, S. I. (1995). "Could do better": *Why children underachieve and what to do about it.* Hoboken, NJ: John Wiley & Sons.

Chapter 7

1. Mandel, H. P., & Marcus, S. I. (1995). "Could do better": *Why children underachieve and what to do about it.*
2. Gold, M. A. & Dahl, R. E. (2011). Using motivational interviewing to facilitate healthier sleep-related behaviors in adolescents. In M. Perlis, M. Aolia, & B. Kuhn (Eds.), *Behavioral treatments for sleep disorders* (pp. 367–380). Amsterdam: Academic Press.
3. Carter, C. (2013, March 11). How to influence your teen, part 1. *Greater Good Magazine.* Retrieved from https://greatergood.berkeley.edu/article/item/how_to_influence_teen_pt1. See also Carter, C. (2013, March 25). Influencing teens and tweeners, part 2. *Greater Good Magazine.* Retrieved from https://greatergood.berkeley.edu/article/item/how_to_influence_teen_pt2.
4. Adams, P. (2014, August 11). The underchallenged 'lazy teenager.' *Wall Street Journal.*

Chapter 8

1. Eiland, L., & Romeo, R. D. (2013). Stress and the developing adolescent brain. *Neuroscience* 249, 162–171.

2. Romeo, R. D. (2013). The teenage brain: The stress response and the adolescent brain. *Current Directions in Psychological Science* 2, 140–145.

3. McMahon, T. (2015, January 4). Inside your teenager's scary brain. *Maclean's.* Retrieved from http://www.macleans.ca/society/life/inside-your-teenagers-scary-brain/.

4. Tough, P. (2012). *How children succeed.*

5. Jensen, F., & Nutt, A. (2016). *The teenage brain: A neuroscientist's survival guide to raising adolescents.* New York: HarperCollins.

6. Shellenbarger, S. (2016, August 9). What teens need most from their parents. *Wall Street Journal.*

7. Suttie, J. (2016, June 1). What adolescents really need from parents. *Greater Good Magazine.* Retrieved from https://greatergood.berkeley.edu/article/item/what_adolescents_really_need_from_parents.

8. Klass, P. (2017, May 22). The science of adolescent sleep. *New York Times.* Retrieved from https://www.nytimes.com/2017/05/22/well/family/the-science-of-adolescent-sleep.html.

Chapter 9

1. Carter, C. (2013, March 11). How to influence your teen, part 1; and Carter, C. (2013, March 25). Influencing teens and tweeners, part 2. *Greater Good Magazine.*

Acknowledgments

My heartfelt thanks to Familius, including Christopher Robbins, David Miles, and Brooke Jorden, for their ideas and support. I am especially fortunate that Lindsay Sandberg agreed to be my editor. Her observations, insights, and practical contributions were invaluable. I also thank Jim Bond for his fresh look at my initial manuscript and his suggestions.

As always, I am grateful to my wife, Shelley, for listening to my ideas and inspiring me in so many ways. I am also grateful to my son Alex for contributing his memories and insights to the book. Thanks to my daughter, Claire, my son, Dylan, and to Chris Short, James Carry, Steve Pollard, and Chuck Tebbetts. I deeply appreciate everyone's encouragement.

About the Author

Mark Luciano, PhD, is a licensed clinical psychologist and qualified school psychologist in California. He is the coauthor of *If Only You Would Change*, which applies principles of the Twelve-Step Program, cognitive behavior therapy, and aspects of Christian spirituality to resolving marital and relationship problems. He has developed a workbook based on the ideas in *If Only You Would Change* and has taught seminars throughout the West. He has appeared as a guest on News 8 San Diego, *Off the Shelf*, and several Christian radio and television programs. Dr. Luciano is the founder of The Family Renewal Center in San Diego, where he has offered marriage and family therapy, helping hundreds of families to resolve issues and advocate for their kids' educational program and success. He lives in San Diego with his wife and his son Dylan, who is in graduate school obtaining his multiple-subject teacher credential.

About Familius

Visit Our Website: www.familius.com

Join Our Family

There are lots of ways to connect with us!

Subscribe to our newsletters at www.familius.com to receive uplifting daily inspiration, essays from our Pater Familius, a free ebook every month, and the first word on special discounts and Familius news.

Get Bulk Discounts

If you feel a few friends and family might benefit from what you've read, let us know and we'll be happy to provide you with quantity discounts. Simply email us at orders@familius.com.

Connect

- Facebook: www.facebook.com/paterfamilius
- Twitter: @familiustalk, @paterfamilius1
- Pinterest: www.pinterest.com/familius
- Instagram: @familiustalk

FAMILIUS

The most important work you ever do will be within the walls of your own home.

CPSIA information can be obtained
at www.ICGtesting.com
Printed in the USA
BVHW070004150319
542725BV00001B/72/P

9 781641 700375